About the Book

Here is the fabulous story of American place-names since Juan Ponce de León put Florida on a blank map in 1513. Author Vernon Pizer tells entertainingly and often hilariously who, how, when, where, and why Americans have established more than 3.5 million names for towns, cities, counties, states, lakes, rivers, mountains, and islands. He shows how any citizen may go on an ego trip when he tries to give identity, meaning, and personality to the place where he lives.

This chronicle of place-names—from Florida in 1513 to the present-day United States of America—is a fascinating amble through our history that delves into forgotten places, forgotten fads, tremendous arguments, and the various lives of a feisty people. America's place-names compose an instance where too many cooks could not spoil the broth. The nation's names were concocted by many hands, each adding its touch of spice, and the blending becomes a feast.

The *Ink, Ark.* of the title refers to a time when a hamlet in a bend of Arkansas' Ouachita River petitioned for a post office. Official Washington, wishing to be democratic, sent each family in the nameless town a questionnaire on which they were to indicate their choice of a name. The form admonished *PLEASE WRITE IN INK*. So a majority of citizens dutifully wrote down *Ink*. Their town, by the way, is only a dozen miles from Pencil Bluff, Arkansas.

Vernon Pizer

Ink, Ark.,
and all that

How American Places Got Their Names

Illustrations by Tom Huffman

G.P. Putnam's Sons   New York

Copyright © 1976 by Vernon Pizer
All rights reserved. Published
simultaneously in Canada by
Longman Canada Limited, Toronto.
SBN: GB-399-61022-7
SBN: TR-399-20532-2

Library of Congress Cataloging in Publication Data

Pizer, Vernon, 1918-
Ink, Ark., and All That

Includes index.
1.   Names, Geographical—United States—Juvenile
literature. 2.   United States—History, Local—
Juvenile literature. [1.   Names, Geographical.
2.   United States—History, Local]   I.   Title.
E155.P59 1976   917.3′001′42   76-13176
Second Impression
PRINTED IN THE UNITED STATES OF AMERICA
10 up

Contents

Acknowledgments

The "all that" of *Ink, Ark., and All That* ranges over a vast expanse of ground, more than any author—no matter his nimbleness or his stamina—could hope to cover perceptively without the help of others along the way. Equity and simple courtesy require that my debt to those who shared their expertise with me be acknowledged, but there are too many to be singled out individually, so I must thank them by groups. To the scores on the staffs of the Board on Geographic Names, the U.S. Geological Survey, the Post Office Department, and other federal agencies, and to the members of historical societies and institutions who generously contributed their wisdom and insights I express my deep appreciation. My gratitude also goes to those who so long ago compiled records and accounts whose yellowing, brittle pages I was able to mine for numerous gleaming nuggets. To offer a complete bibliography of all the published works I consulted would be as overwhelming a task as naming the individuals who offered their help. But I would be remiss if I did not mention at least the more than fifty volumes that constitute the federal government's admirable *American Guide Series,* and George R. Stewart's classic *Names on the Land.*

On a more personal note, I must thank Marguerite for her forbearance, understanding, and endurance throughout the long period of this book's gestation.

VERNON PIZER

But these are deeds which should not pass away,
And names that must not wither.

—LORD BYRON

1

What's in a Name?

In the spring of 1513 three small ships flying the flag of Spain sailed through the Caribbean Sea. Setting a northwesterly course, they penetrated ever farther into waters that no European explorers had entered before them.

Early on the afternoon of April 2, the vessels were moving smartly before a steady breeze, sailing bow-to-stern in column. Juan Ponce de León, commander of the expedition, was on the deck of the lead ship speculating on what might lie in the watery unknown ahead. Suddenly, from the crow's nest high on the mast, the lookout's voice rang out: "Land!"

Excitement swept through the little fleet. Differences in rank forgotten, officers and men alike—Ponce de León among them—crowded the rails to stare in the direction the lookout was pointing. Slowly, too slowly to suit the impatient sailors, the land began to rise up out of the sea as the breeze carried the vessels closer to shore.

With the coastal features becoming clear, the men aboard the three craft could see that they were sailing into a green, lush world. Along the length of the shoreline dense foliage and thick woodlands stretched back from the broad, sandy beach. This was a fertile and fruitful place—of that there could be no doubt. Surveying the unfolding scene, Ponce de León was immensely pleased. His discovery would surely win him praise, and material rewards as well, in the court of his king, His Catholic Majesty, Ferdinand of Aragón.

Dropping anchor in shallow water, Ponce de León ordered a small boat lowered and prepared to go ashore with the landing party to claim the territory on behalf of Spain. Then he paused at the rail, deep in thought as he contemplated the land, realizing that he would have to give the place a name as a part of the process of declaring it a Spanish possession. What should be call it? What would be suitable, both for the land itself and for the ears of his king? The chaplain of the expedition offered a suggestion. Reminding Juan that it was a holy day, the time of the Feast of Flowers, he proposed that the land be named for that festival. Juan weighed the suggestion, rolling it over his tongue a time or two to get the sound of it, and he found merit in it. Nodding his agreement, he climbed down to the waiting boat.

When the boat grounded on the beach Ponce de León stepped ashore. Then, with the chaplain at one side and the color-bearer holding the royal standard at the other, he claimed the land for Ferdinand, naming it Florida for *Pascua Florida,* the Feast of Flowers. With that act Juan Ponce de León created the oldest geographic place-name of European origin still in use in the United States.

Since that historic day in 1513 when Ponce de León put Florida on the map, more than 3.5 million additional place-names have been established across the country. Marching over the length and breadth of the nation like a vast, relentless army, this multitude of names has given identity, meaning, personality to villages and towns and cities, to counties and states, to lakes, rivers and creeks, to mountains and valleys, to deserts, swamps and plains, to islands and seashores.

Yet the place-name seldom rates a second thought. It is there, it is used, and it is unheralded as the marvelously useful tool it has become. Perhaps the geographic name is a victim of its own success. Perhaps because it serves its function effectively, consistently, and readily, it is inevitable that it be taken for granted.

But try to spend an entire day without once using a place-name and you appreciate the vital role it plays. It isn't impossible to get through the day without calling on a place-name for help, but it isn't easy—not if you turn to a newspaper or a map or listen to a news broadcast, write a letter or make a long-distance phone call, talk about the Green Bay Packers or about surfing in Waikiki or skiing in Squaw Valley, grouse about smog in Los Angeles or fumes in Pittsburgh, order a bucket of the Colonel's Kentucky Fried Chicken, speculate on what the politicians are up to in Washington, or look for the Nashville sound among the disks in the record shop. It takes real effort—and a changed life-style—to make it through a whole day without leaning on any of the 3.5 million place-names for support.

No question about it, the place-name that we take for granted is one of our most essential communication tools, in one way or another sustaining almost everything we do. So thoroughly are places-names a part of everyday living that they have even crept into our language in ways that the geographic namers had never planned.

Hear "Conestoga" and you think of the covered wagons in which the pioneers forged westward, but the word began as the name of the town in which the wagons were first designed and built: Conestoga, Pennsylvania. Hear "baked Alaska" and you don't assume a heat wave has hit our northernmost state; you picture a meringue-covered dessert. Hear "tuxedo" and you think immediately of a formal dinner-jacket, but the word was created as the name of a town: Tuxedo, New York. It was there, in the 1880's, that the wealthy men of the town fell into the habit of dressing for dinner in identical black, satin-lapeled jackets which became known by the name of the town where they were invented.

Place-names have even spilled over from language to "slan-guage." If we think something is nonsense we label it "bunk" without realizing that this slang expression is a geographic place-name. It goes back to 1820 when Congressman Felix Walker, from Buncombe County, North Carolina, rose in Congress to deliver a long-winded, pointless speech. When Walker finally sat down, another congressman asked him why he had wasted their time with such nonsense. "But I wasn't speaking for myself; I was speaking for Buncombe," Walker replied. The incident was too amusing to remain on Capitol Hill, and increasing numbers of people began using "buncombe" as a synonym for non-sense. In time it became abbreviated to "bunk," immortalizing a North Carolina county in American slang.

So great is the influence of place-names that a whole field of scholarly research—toponymy—is devoted to them. By nature and by training, toponymists are suspicious: they never take a place-name at face value. Instead, they persist in digging be-neath the surface to discover what may be hidden there. As they probe, they continually seek clues to the answers to a series of questions they always have in mind. When, by whom, and why was that particular name selected? Does it come from a foreign language, and if it does, what does it mean in that language? Was that place ever called something different at an earlier time? If so, what was its former name and why was the change made? Finally, the toponymist wants to know the boundaries of the place referred to: in other words, where does that place-name end and the next one begin?

Often the settlement of a legal dispute can hinge on a name. Suppose that a farmer has been granted the right to grow crops in "Green Valley" at the foot of "Eagle Mountain," how high up the side of the valley has he the right to plant his crops? Which is the same way as asking at what point Green Valley becomes Eagle Mountain. Trained toponymists, analyzing appropriate records and documents, can help figure out the answer.

Not only lawyers, but also historians, educators, engineers, surveyors, geographers, geologists, government agencies, even sociologists and anthropologists turn to toponymists for help with many of their problems. This is because in the hands of the skillful a place-name is much more than merely an identifying signpost; it is a vast storehouse of varied information. Handled properly, a place-name becomes a servant of many different masters.

Toponymists analyzed place-names of Indian origin to discover the specific tribal language from which each was formed. Then—by charting the locations of all names coming from the same language—they were able to outline the precise area inhabited by each tribe before the white men arrived and dispersed them. Going further, they milked from Indian names an understanding of what the country was like in those distant days of the past. For example, because a city that developed in what is now Illinois adopted for itself the old Indian name for the area, toponymists learned that wild onions grew there. The city is Chicago, Indian for "place where wild onions grow." Similarly, they learned that great herds of buffalo once roamed southwest of Chicago because a city built there assumed the existing place-name— Peoria—and Peoria means "place of fat beasts." Peorians should be grateful that their city founders did not adopt the English translation of the name. Who among us would admit that he comes from the place of fat beasts?

Betsie—not a girl, but a place in Michigan—baffled toponymists for a long time. After digging diligently to learn how and why that place-name came into being, they finally uncovered a map of the area that French explorers had drawn two centuries earlier. On their map the Frenchmen had labelled a small river *Aux Becs Scies,* "at the sawfish snouts." Continuing to dig for the rest of the story, the investigators discovered that English-speaking settlers who later arrived to carve out homesteads found the French words more of a challenge to their spelling ability than they cared to accept. Taking the easy way out, they simplified *Aux Becs Scies* to Betsie. So because "place-name detectives" tackled the mystery of Betsie it was discovered that sawfish—odd creatures with long, blade-like snouts—once swam in Michigan waters.

Not all of the puzzles reach back so far into the past. Some of the newer place-names contribute their share of mystery. The pups of Alaska are a case in point.

Examine a map of Alaska printed after 1900 and you find on it places like Big Pup, Brown Pup and Crooked Pup. In each instance the "pup" in the name indicates a ravine—a narrow, deep valley through which a river flows. But why "pup"? Why such a curious word to signify a ravine when never before had any geographer used that word in that way? The trail eventually led toponymists to one Miller, a man whose first name is unknown today.

Miller was a prospector working a claim in the Alaska gold-fields in the 1890s. His only companion was his dog. One summer Miller's dog had a litter of puppies and, to keep them from wandering off, the prospector penned them in a small ravine near his cabin where he could keep a protective eye on them. Becoming accustomed to seeing Miller's puppies penned in their little valley, other prospectors took to calling the ravine "Miller's Pup." The name caught on and when a new map of the area was printed it identified the ravine officially as Miller's Pup. After that, it became a goldfield custom to call a ravine a pup; the practice even crossed the border into Canada. Without intending it, Miller and his puppies had added one more colorful note to the world of place-names.

But the place-name is more than a key that unlocks doors to the past, more than a device to enable people to communicate intelligently about places. It is also pretty much whatever you want to make of it—a bag of tricks, a treasure-chest of delightful surprises, a jack-of-all-trades. The truth is that there is a special quality to American place-names, a uniqueness that is all their own and that gives them a distinctive versatility.

You can munch on place-names like Egg Harbor, Bacon Park,

Hominy, Toast, Whitefish, Oyster, Bean City, Wild Rice, Turkey and Chili; finish off your gluttony in Pie Town, New Mexico, and Hot Coffee, Mississippi; and then—as a wise precaution—check in at Doctortown, Georgia, or at least pause in Seltzer, Pennsylvania.

A place-name excursion into the human anatomy? How about Great Neck, Big Arm, Finger, Footville, Elbow Lake, Bowlegs, Kneeland, Chest Springs and Bone Cave? For a touch of variety you might add such towns as Blue Eye, Mouth of Wilson and Brainy Boro.

A place-name weather report could include the towns of Rains, Cloudy, Coolville, Stormville, Sunshine, Snowflake, Windy, Frost, Warm Lake and Hot Springs. Those turned on by more violent weather can do their thing in Thunderbolt, Georgia; Hurricane, Utah; Cyclone, Pennsylvania; and Tornado, West Virginia.

Feeling depressed? Among places that buoy up the dispirited are Smile, Kentucky; Jolly, Texas; Happy Jack, Arizona; What Cheer, Iowa; Hop Bottom and Scalp Level in Pennsylvania; and Goose Pimple Junction, Nuttsville, and Tightsqueeze in Virginia.

Those with empty pockets may find enrichment in Nickelsville, Virginia; Dime Box, Texas; Dames Quarter, Maryland; Dollar Bay, Michigan; Money, Mississippi; or Cash, Arkansas. For sports fans there are Polo, Missouri; Ball Club, Minnesota; Golf, Illinois; and Umpire, Arkansas. Music lovers can listen to the sounds of Fiddletown, California; Fife, Texas; Tuba City, Arizona; and Drums and Moosic, Pennsylvania. Car buffs may be attracted to Cylinder, Iowa; Auto, West Virginia; Tire Hill, Pennsylvania; Gas, Kansas; or Oil City, Louisiana; and in the event of a breakdown they will be grateful for Tow, Texas. Circusgoers will be pleased with Tiger, Washington; Elephant Butte, New Mexico; Red Lion, Pennsylvania; Dwarf, Kentucky; and Tarzan, Texas; while the clothes-conscious can shop in Coats, Kansas; Suitland, Maryland; Belt, Montana; Tie Siding, Wyoming; and Vest or Hi Hat, Kentucky.

That is the way it goes in the lively world of place-names—something for everyone, for every taste, and for every occasion. No matter what comes to mind, somewhere among the millions of place-names that freckle the broad face of America it is bound to exist. In her place-names one can even find the hope and the promise of the nation: Fair Play, Missouri, Justice, West Virginia; Unity, Wisconsin; and Freedom, New Hampshire. But to scan the long list of American place-names just to squeeze from it its chuckles or its surprises of its oddities is to miss the best it has to offer. The real treasure in the rich lode of place-names is not so much what the names say but rather how and why they came to say it. Behind each name there is a story—sometimes amusing, sometimes illuminating a forgotten fragment of history, sometimes inspiring, sometimes mournful, but always revealing and never dull.

2

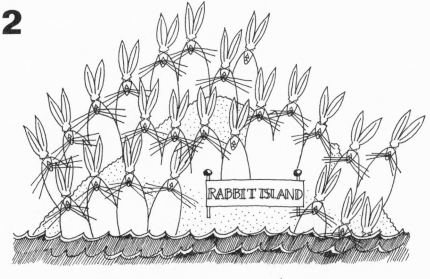

Thorns in the Thicket

During the colonial period that culminated in the Revolutionary War, five European powers competed for a slice of the American pie: Spain, France, England, Holland, and Sweden. Spain had an enormous appetite, laying claim to a broad horizontal band of the continent stretching east-west from Florida to California. France's land hunger was more vertical—the French staked out a north-south claim covering the length of the Mississippi River valley system, plus a few bites in the east. England chose to digest the Atlantic coastal flank of the continent. The most modest in their appetites were the Dutch and the Swedes who chewed on the areas through which the Hudson and Delaware Rivers flow.

Probing the regions over which they sought to achieve domination, seeking to solidify and strengthen their claims, the Europeans established settlements in places that seemed to them to be economically promising or to offer strategic advantage. And for each settlement they established they created an identifying place-name. Like the "Kilroy Was Here" signs that were to proliferate at a much later date, the place-names were tangible markers of a presence. But Kilroy was only a mythical character and those who frivolously posted signs in his behalf simply intended them as humorous claims that the legendary Kilroy had passed that way. There was nothing frivolous in the intentions of the colonial powers. Their place-names were meant to record their physical presence and to justify their claims in the areas they coveted.

For many of the early explorers—and for the settlers who followed in their wake—place-naming was a do-it-yourself proposition, with the names being selected by them according to their personal views of what seemed to be most suitable at the moment. What sometimes struck them as most appropriate was to flatter their own egos by naming places after themselves or after members of their families. However, aside from these forays into do-it-yourselfism or the honor-yourselfism, each of the colonizing powers had its own national style of naming places.

The Spanish, so steeped in Catholicism, sprinkled ecclesiastical names across their New World lands like priests sprinkling holy water. From the Spanish came such names as St. Augustine in Florida; San Jose, Santa Barbara, and Sacramento ("sacrament") in California; and Corpus Christi ("Body of Christ") in Texas. And one must not forget the wonderfully mouth-filling La Villa Real de Santa Cruz de los Españoles Mexicanos del Rey Nuestro Señor Don Carlos Segundo—The Royal Town of the Holy Cross of the Spanish Mexicans of the King Our Master Carlos II. Dramatically streamlined into a pale shadow of itself, that name continues today as simply Santa Cruz, New Mexico.

The English were more attuned to the Crown than to the Cross, usually honoring their aristocracy by naming places after British nobles or after the estates on which the nobles lived back in England. From the English came names like

Annapolis for Queen Anne, Amherst for Lord Jeffrey Amherst, Shrewsbury for the Earl of Shrewsbury, Great Barrington for Viscount Barrington, Yorktown for the Duke of York, and Rockingham for the Marquess of Rockingham.

The down-to-earth Dutch were plainspoken and direct in choosing their place-names. From the solid, matter-of-fact Dutch came Kaatskill—later Anglicized to Catskill—because wildcats ("kaats") used to frequent the creek ("kill") at that New York site. Elsewhere in New York it was the Dutch who named an island Konijn Eilandt ("Rabbit Island") because it was well populated by those creatures; and the rabbits have long since disappeared from the Anglicized Coney Island. The Swedes, because the area they controlled was so small and the duration of their stay as a colonial power in America so brief (1633 to 1655), had no opportunity to engage in any significant amount of place-naming and thus had no chance to display a distinctive style.

The French were the butterflies among the colonial place-namers, flitting back and forth among naming systems as the spirit seemed to move them. Sometimes, like the Spanish, they chose religious names such as Sainte Genevieve, Saint Louis, and Saint Joseph in Missouri. Sometimes, like the English, they honored their nobility with names like Nouvelle Orléans (later to become New Orleans) for the Duke of Orléans. Sometimes, like the Dutch, they became matter-of-fact and chose names like Terre Haute ("high ground") in Indiana for the elevated position of the location, and like Baie Vert for the green vegetation surrounding that Wisconsin bay and which is now known as Green Bay.

And sometimes they took off on their own, coining a name simply because it suited their fancy. This is what happened when French trappers, passing through the broad prairie where the Mississippi and Wisconsin Rivers join, became familiar with the dominant local Indian chief and discovered him to be an unsavory character. To express their feelings toward the chief, the trappers nicknamed him *Le Chien* ("The Dog"). Later, when three Frenchmen established a trading post there that was one day to flourish into a city, they immortalized the derisive nickname by calling their settlement *Prairie du Chien*.

Although each of the colonial powers followed its own inclinations in the matter of geographical christenings, none of them could completely ignore the place-names that already existed in the region it was claiming. After all, for hundreds of years before the advent of the white man the red man had been planting his own names on the land and they could not be blinked away as though they had never existed. So the Europeans preserved many of the Indian names they found but they did so in ways that were distinguished by error and misunderstanding.

The confusion and mistakes were inevitable, inescapable. If the basic reason has to be compressed into a single word that word must surely be "language." Language is supposed to be the glue that brings people together and holds them fast, that bonds them to each other in common communication and understanding. In colonial America, however, the glue came unstuck; it didn't bind people, but separated them. The root of the problem was simply too much language in the New World. There were so many different tribal languages and dialects that usually Indians from one section of the country had to resort to gestures to try to communicate with Indians from another section. Furthermore, the various foreign languages the whites brought from Europe made a difficult situation worse by creating new and greater barriers to understanding. Without a common language communication in early America was a hit-or-miss proposition, with misses at least as frequent as hits—and often more frequent.

A white man, wanting to know the name of a river, might point to it and ask an Indian in a language he understood poorly or not at all, "What is that?" The Indian, trying his best to grasp the sense of the question and not quite succeeding, might look at the waterway toward which his questioner was pointing and say, "Big fish." Whereupon the white man would carefully record Big Fish River as its name.

But while this little play was being acted, a similar scene might be unfolding with a different cast of characters miles downstream. There the supposed name of the river might emerge as "Place where the deer drink." So the records might list two (or more) different names for the same thing. While each claimed to be accurate, all might be wrong.

A glance at a map of Tennessee shows, for example, the Hatchie River. Early explorers mapping that section of the country asked local Indians what they called the waterway. Trying their best to be cooperative, though they could not understand the words of the white man, the Indians took their cue from his gesture and said, "Hatchie." The whites conscientiously lettered Hatchie River on their maps, and so it remains today. But hatchie simply means "river," so Hatchie River is a redundant "river river," which is no name at all.

Compounding all the difficulties was the fact there was at that time no written Indian language, only many spoken languages. This meant that every time a white wanted to record an Indian place-name—or what was assumed an Indian place-name—he had to decide how he ought to spell it in order to best reproduce in written form the sounds the Indian made in pronouncing it. But each European spelled sounds according to the rules of his own native language. Thus, a Frenchman, an Englishman, a Spaniard, and a Dutchman would each write his own version of an Indian name and each would end up with a different spelling.

Even when unwitting misunderstanding was not a factor, the European often could not resist the temptation to tamper with Indian names. His itch to switch is readily explained when one considers that, viewed solely through white's eyes, many Indian names almost begged to be altered and modified. Almost always they involved guttural, awkward sounds that were difficult for European tongues to master comfortably and European pens to write readily. So, to make things easier for himself, the European was quick to shorten and revise Indian place-names to eliminate the most awkward pronunciations and simplify the writing.

Dutch colonists in New Jersey, for instance, performed linguistic surgery on Hapoaken-hocking ("Land of the tobacco pipe") to change it to Hoboken. Far to the west of Hoboken, in what is now Arizona, Spanish missionaries came to a small Indian village called Stjukshon ("At the foot of a black hill") by its residents and eventually they altered it to Tucson. A Lake Erie bay called San-doos-tee ("At the cold water") by the Indians was changed to Sandouske by the French, and a century later Englishmen continued the process by modifying Sandouske to Sandusky. Other Englishmen, establishing themselves in 1622 in Rhode Island, at a place called Miswosakit ("At the steep hill") promptly corrupted it into Woonsocket.

In countless instances, in every part of the land, the whites jiggled and juggled place-names to reshape them into something less Indian and more European in form. This Europeanizing of Indian names squeezed much of the juice from them, leaving them limp and dry. In their original form they had been robust words meaningful by describing an event or circumstance associated with the site, but in altered form they had no clear meaning. Norwaake was an Indian place-name meaning "Point of land" and thus it described its physical situation jutting out into a river. When English-speaking colonists settled that Connecticut location in 1650 they "civilized" the name to Norwalk which, of course, means nothing despite the mistaken assertions of some that it is an abbreviation of "north walk."

A few hundred miles up the coast from Norwalk is a Maine town called Poland, which seems to be just about as European as an American place-name can be. In reality, it is nothing of the sort. It commemorates an Indian chief whose name was closely linked to the site where settlers established their town. The trouble was that the settlers could not resist the urge to graft a Europeanizing *d* to the end of Chief Polan's name so they wound up with something that is actually neither Indian nor European and has no real meaning.

Sometimes, thinking to retain an original Indian name and yet to enjoy the familiarity of his own language, the white translated the name into whichever European language he happened to speak. This did little to reduce confusion because whites who often understood Indian languages imperfectly could usually be counted on to translate them imperfectly. In Nebraska, for instance, English-speaking settlers established a community on the bank of a creek which, because of the soft, melodic murmuring of the gently flowing water, the Indians called Nigahoe, meaning "rustling water." Deciding to retain the existing placename but in its English form, the settlers mistranslated it into Weeping Water. Although it was no less poetic than rustling water, "weeping water" was not only a false translation but was also unsuited to the situation. There was nothing sad or tearful about the creek; it had been murmuring its gently rustling, pleasantly soothing melody until a flawed interpretation changed its tune, at least on paper. It is "nihoage," not "nigahoe," that translates into "weeping water."

But if the whites were quick to tamper with Indian placenames, they were often just as quick to give each other's placenames the same sort of treatment. Maps compiled by early Spanish explorers probing the Gulf coast of Alabama indicated a site called Mauvila for the local Mauvila tribe of Indians. Later, in the 1600s, a small French force moved in and established a fortified post at Mauvila. They were willing enough to retain the established name, but, to make it clear they had supplanted the Spanish at Mauvila, they altered it to the more French-sounding Mobile. (One group of Spaniards did its own tampering with a Spanish name. One of the earliest European place-names in America was San Iago, given to a bay in California in 1542 by Cabrillo, the first white to sail along the west coast of the continent. Spanish colonists who followed him founded a settlement they named for the bay, corrupting it into San Diego.)

The French got a taste of their own medicine several hundred miles north of Mauvila/Mobile. There, in what is now Arkansas, a party of French surveyors had come across a lovely spot covered with a pink carpeting of flowering sumac. They promptly named the site Sumac-couvert, "sumac-covered." English settlers who years later founded a town there could not work up any enthusiasm for living in a place that bore a French name so they Anglicized Sumac-couvert into Smackover.

If Smackover goes to extreme lengths to mask its origin, there is another name that belongs in the same league. In the 1700s Spanish explorers in what would eventually become Colorado reached a river where they were massacred by Comanches. To mark the tragedy, Spanish authorities named the river El Rio de Las Animas Perdidas en Purgatorio, "the river of souls lost in purgatory." French trappers later shortened the long, storytelling name and gave it a French accent by reducing it to Purgatoire. Still later, however, Americans made Purgatoire's accent unmistakably American by altering it to Picketwire.

In colonial Connecticut Dutch surveyors mapping land as a step in consolidating Holland's claim over it chose Rodenberghen, "red hills," to designate the russet bluffs overlooking the mouth of the Quinnipiac River. The English authorities, trying to steal a march on the Dutch and to outflank their claim, moved quickly to establish their own colonists at the site. They obviously would not accept the Dutch name because to retain it would be to concede that the Dutch had a legitimate claim to the area. So, using a place-name to support a political objective, the English discarded Rodenberghen and supplanted it with Quinnipiac. Finding they were little happier with an Indian place-name than a Dutch one, they dropped Quinnipiac in 1640 for a name that had the solid sound of England in it: New Haven.

Dutch names were frequent victims in the tug-of-war between England and Holland over American land. Among the many Dutch casualties were Breukelen, which became Brooklyn, and New Amsterdam, which became New York. In New Jersey a finger of land called Ompoge, "Large, flat land," by the Indians was corrupted by the Dutch into Amboy; after the English displaced the Dutch into 1669, they altered it to Perth Amboy. This gave them an opportunity to honor the Earl of Perth and at the same time swap the Dutch sound of the name for something English.

Place-names sprouted indiscriminately in the fertile soil of early America—names honoring the Church or the aristocracy or places back in the Old World, names describing the appearance of a site or an event that had transpired there, names conceived in error or an attempt at self-flattery, names that tampering hands had misshaped. As a result, the growth became entangled and matted. The first to realize it wise to start some pruning in the developing thicket were the authorities in Massachusetts Bay Colony.

On September 7, 1630, the Massachusetts General Court was convened to regulate the place-naming process within its jurisdiction. First of all, the court made it clear that henceforth all place-names in the colony would require its approval before they could become official. Then, turning its attention to the matter of names already in use, the court weighed the merits of each and found a number that did not measure up to its idea of suitability. Among the changes the magistrates ordered during that and later sessions, Assawam became Ipswich, Musketequid became Concord, and Trimountain became Boston. (Although this was only some ten years after the *Mayflower* had brought the first Pilgrims to Massachusetts it was already Boston's second name change; before it had become Trimountain, the site was called Shamut—"fountain"—by the Indians.)

The General Court was firm in ordering its changes, and, though there was muttered resentment, they were accepted. But when the magistrates sought to eliminate Marblehead they ran into a storm of protest that refused to die away. The Marble-headers were so belligerent in defense of their name that in the end the magistrates caved in and allowed them to keep it.

Massachusetts was the sole colony taking steps to regularize and control the place-naming process. Elsewhere on the continent the other colonies were permitting names to continue to spring into existence both in accordance with their own varied customs and—often—in response to haphazard, individual whim. This was providing the makings of future headaches for the nation that would one day emerge. At the same time, it was providing the colorful, individualistic tiles that make American place-names an unorthodox, fascinating mosaic.

3

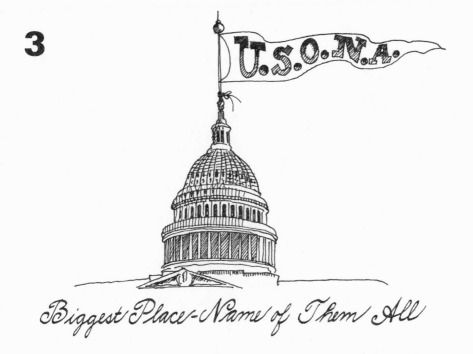

Biggest Place-Name of Them All

America had not been the first choice as a place-name. The earliest European explorers and the earliest chronicles recording their findings had all referred to the newly discovered land as the Indies, or the West Indies, or the New World. If there was uncertainty as to which label to apply, there was similar uncertainty as to exactly what was being labeled.

Christopher Columbus was still convinced on his deathbed in 1506 that in 1492 he had reached the outlying portions of Asia known as the Indies; up to his last breath he referred to it by that title. John Cabot sailed to what is now Newfoundland in 1497 and reported that he had reached China. After he completed an extended probing along its coastline in 1501–1502, Amerigo Vespucci declared the recently discovered land mass to be a New World.

Back in Europe, Martin Waldseemüller, a prominent German scholar and geographer, evaluated all of the reports, opinions, and guesses. After his careful winnowing, he constructed and published a map in 1507 depicting the land as a new continent. A primary source of his data had been a detailed account by Amerigo Vespucci describing his findings on his long voyage of exploration. To repay the debt he felt he owed Vespucci, Waldseemüller labeled the continent America, the feminine form of Amerigo. Circulating widely through Europe, the Waldseemüller map attracted lively attention and gathered converts to the continent theory. America gained acceptance as its place-name. (But for at least a century longer, the Spanish and Portuguese were holdouts continuing to speak in terms of the Indies, the West Indies, and the New World. Eventually they were forced to fall into line because they could not forever remain out of step with the rest of the world.)

Waldseemüller was a good geographer but not infallible. His map contained a serious flaw in that it depicted America as a single elongated continent. In 1538 Gerardus Mercator, a famed Flemish cartographer, corrected the error by indicating that America was in reality two continents. He extended the place-name to both continents, prefixing it in the one case with "north" and in the other with "south."

North America was now a place-name on the map but it was a skeleton with no flesh on the bones. Whether written simply as America or as the more proper North America, it was still only a mark on a map, a word to indicate an enormous, ill-defined, little-known continent. It was not yet a place-name in the truest sense, a designation with real meaning, something the gathering colonists could identify with and attach themselves to in a personal way. America or North America, to them it was simply a tool of the geographer's trade, a convenient handle for cartographers to grasp as a way of dealing with a vast, vague land.

The only major place-name that held real meaning for the colonists, the one they could identify with, was the one designating the specific colony in which they lived. It represented something they could relate to as individuals, something they could understand and feel a part of. The name of the continent had not assumed the ability to draw the colonists together and command their loyalty, as had the names of their respective colonies. So the colonies went their separate ways under separate names, guided by their own authorities. Each was independent of the others and was, in fact, frequently at odds with them. They identified, not with one another, but with the homeland back in Europe.

Only among the English colonies occupying the Eastern seaboard was there any feeling of kinship. Here the differences were fewer and the frictions less abrasive. Here were natural bonds growing out of a shared heritage, a common language, geographical proximity (although this also sometimes created dissension), and the allegiance that each owed the English Crown.

It was the English settlers who made the first attempt to create a place-name and a political structure that crossed colonial borders—New England. As a name, New England came into existence almost exactly one hundred years after Waldseemüller coined America. In 1616, Captain John Smith of Virginia published maps and reports revealing his findings on exploratory voyages he had made northward along the coast during the previous two years. In the reports and on the maps he referred to the region he had probed as New England, the first time anyone had used that term. As Smith employed it, the name had little real significance since the region to which it was applied was unclear and uncertain.

In 1643 New England assumed a more precise meaning when Massachusetts, Plymouth, Connecticut, and New Haven formed the New England Confederation as a cooperative body to support their joint, intercolonial interests. Thus the initial and tentative movement along the arduous, winding road from individual, separate colonies toward an eventual national structure and national place-name commenced with the New England Confederation.

Although the Confederation lasted for only forty years, it was not without its accomplishments while it did exist. But when the Confederation passed from the scene in 1684 New England reverted once again to being an uncertain place-name. It could not in the future become a title for the English colonies as a whole because it had, during the life of the Confederacy, been too closely linked with only a few of the colonies in the northern sector of the seaboard. And even those colonies removed from the name whatever concrete meaning it had when they had allowed the Confederation to expire. So New England became largely a state of mind, a generalization. There was still no name with which the colonies as a whole could identify, none that could exert a cohesive influence over them.

Then, in 1684, a remarkable Bostonian named Cotton Mather filled the void. Mather was a distinguished clergyman and intellectual whose reputation extended well beyond the borders of his native Massachusetts. His words were listened to attentively throughout the English colonies, his views were respected. When Mather wrote of his fellow colonists in 1684 as "Americans" it was the first recorded use of that word as a term for those who had emigrated from the other side of the Atlantic. It had a profound effect on them. It stimulated them to think of themselves for the first time as Americans and to think of America as a place-name that was more than merely a convenient geographic device. America became a name that represented a homeland. The concept of Americans as a separate and distinct people and of America as a cohesive place with a destiny of its own began to take hold and flourish.

The concept was given fresh impetus—unwittingly and unintentionally—by the British authorities themselves during the War of Jenkins' Ear, 1739 to 1742, which pitted the English against the Spanish. In that war 3,000 colonial troops serving under their own officers fought alongside the British regulars. During the conflict the British referred officially to the colonial troops as Americans instead of "provincials," as they always had in the past. This implicit admission by British officialdom that its colonial subjects had been cast in a different mold helped to solidify the colonists' sense of a mutual identity setting them apart from others.

The colonies and the citizens along the eastern seaboard were developing a consciousness of themselves as a distinct people. With it came growing irritation with dictation from abroad that ignored their wishes and needs. The chafing began to flicker into sparks of rebellion. The flicker smoldered, spread, flared up, and created among many Americans a need they perceived for a joint stand against an England they considered a menace to their welfare.

These rebellious Americans felt a joint political structure was needed to develop and direct their resistance against England. This led to establishment of the Continental Congress in 1774. It now was apparent that a common name was also required.

The first name that came into general use emerged naturally from the circumstances that had produced the need for it: the united stand of the colonies against the mother country. That situation created its own title: the United Colonies. Then, to give it a geographical location, the name was broadened to include two different versions of it: the United Colonies of America, and the United Colonies of North America. Either form was used in accordance with the preference of the user. However, there was widespread dissatisfaction with both versions. Neither was considered to be really adequate because each was, in effect, a denial of the mood and the purpose of the rebellion. After all, citizens were taking up arms to enforce their decision that they were no longer colonials subject to dictation from England. How could they, then, employ a title that clearly affirmed that they were citizens of colonies? "Colonies" had to be eliminated from the name. So political leaders began to speak of "states."

Because old habits die hard the transition from "colonies" to "states" was not accomplished in a sudden and complete break with past usage. For a time both terms were used, and sometimes in almost the same breath. Even the resolution presented to the Second Continental Congress in the summer of 1776 by Richard Henry Lee of Virginia said that "the United Colonies are, and of right ought to be, free and independent states."

The first formal document to make the official national name unmistakably clear was—with superb appropriateness—the Declaration of Independence. That document, movingly drafted by Thomas Jefferson and adopted by Congress on July 4, 1776, proclaimed that "We, therefore, the Representatives of the United States of America. . . ." According to legend, it was Benjamin Franklin who had penned in the words "United States of America" as the original draft was being polished and refined prior to its adoption by Congress. Whoever the actual author may have been, the nation-in-the-making had found an official name. Now it set about the arduous task of making itself a nation in fact as well as in name.

After the outcome of the Revolution had confirmed the creation of the country and peace had been restored to the land, people had time again to think about their national name. Doubts set in. Much was found wrong with the nation's name. "The name was an umbrella raised over our heads and it brought us together out of the rain," some said. "It served its purpose effectively but now the purpose has changed. Now we need a name for all seasons, one we can live with comfortably for all time."

Many complained that the name was too long and unwieldy, too lacking in the instant recognition of such short, pithy national place-names as France, Spain, Sweden, or even the country the colonies had rebelled against—England. Furthermore, the critics said, it was not a name that could be personalized for its citizens in the same convenient, natural way that natives of France, Spain, Sweden, or England could be referred to as French, Spanish, Swedish, or English. Instead, they said, the citizens of the new nation had simply a name that identified them as Americans—citizens of a continent that they shared with others—in the same way that Europeans identified inhabitants of Europe but not citizens of a specific European country.

Some complained that "United States of America" lacked warmth, that it sounded less like a nation of living, breathing human beings than it did like an incorporation of cold, depersonalized, mechanical units. It might be a fit name for a company, they said, but not for a country. Many pointed out that it was not even a precise and accurate name since there were both a North and a South America rather than a single America as the name clearly and erroneously implied. It was, in fact, because of that lack of geographical exactness that the treaty signed with France in 1778 had attempted to overcome the flaw by employing United States of North America as the national name.

As rumblings of discontent over the way in which the nation styled itself echoed through the land, several suggestions were put forth. During the waning days of the eighteenth century and the opening days of the nineteenth, when public disaffection for the national title was persistent and loud, the proposed substitute that enjoyed the broadest measure of public support was Columbia. There were a number of sound reasons partisans of Columbia could cite to bolster their choice. They pointed out that the name had a legitimate historic connection with the land it would designate since it would honor the man who was credited with having discovered it. They emphasized it was short, distinctive, simple to write and pronounce, and lent itself conveniently to tranformation into a suitable term for citizens of the nation: Columbians. Finally, they argued that it was already well established as a familiar and completely acceptable placename since a few American towns had already styled themselves Columbia.

Columbia did have a lot to commend it and an army of boosters beat the drums for its acceptance. But other proposed names claimed their own loyal legions of supporters, each legion convinced it had the best remedy to cure the shortcomings in the national name. One group pushed hard for Fredonia, a Latinized version of "freedom." Its partisans boasted that Fredonia distilled into a single word the idealistic essence of the nation, the very foundation on which it had been conceived and built: freedom and liberty. Its detractors, and there were many, condemned Fredonia as an artificial word manufactured by a language mechanic and lacking the kind of historic link to the land that could be claimed for a name such as Columbia. When it became apparent that the nation would not become Fredonia, a town in New York adopted it for its name. Later, other towns borrowed the name from Fredonia, New York.

A radically different proposal that was put forth anticipated by a century or so the fondness modern society has developed for acronyms—words formed from the initial letters of other words, like NASA, WAC, UNESCO, and NATO. This suggestion was that the nation be called USONA, the acronym for United States of North America. The citizens of USONA would become Usonians. But the proposal was unpopular and never achieved really serious consideration.

Not so readily dismissed was the proposal brought forth by Washington Irving. Here, after all, was no crackpot. Irving was an admired, respected writer who had attracted a large following, and his opinions carried weight. From the fertile mind of Irving came not one, but two possiblities for a new national name: Appalachia and Allegania. Even-handed about the matter, he favored neither one over the other, satisfied that either would be a marked improvement over United States of America.

There was no denying that both Appalachia and Allegania were distinctive, that they rolled off the tongue pleasantly enough, and that each had a New World flavor despite its Old World Latinized ending. Each also enjoyed a historic link to the land it was intended for.

Of the two, Appalachia had roots going back farther into the past. It had its beginnings in an expedition commanded by Panfilo de Narváez that sailed from Spain in 1527 to seek gold in Florida. The following spring Narváez dropped anchor near present-day Tampa and led a group inland in an arduous, futile search for treasure. The place where he gave up the search, before sailing on to Mexico, was an Indian village called Apalachee.

Some years later other Spanish explorers probing up from the Florida peninsula recalled the name that Narváez had recorded and inserted it on their maps to indicate the little-known, mountainous region north of Florida. Eventually that name, modified in spelling from Apalachee, was pinned down more narrowly to indicate a specific mountain range: the Appalachian Mountains.

A century and a half after the fruitless Narváez expedition in Florida, a survey party mapping a section of western Pennsylvania discovered a major river. They lettered Allegheny on their charts as its name, forming it from an Indian word meaning "good river." Later the same name was extended to cover the mountain range that paralleled the river for much of its course. Still later, in 1799, a region around the river became Allegheny County, Pennsylvania. So when people speculated over a possible successor to United States of America, Allegania—like Appalachia—was already familiar.

The debates droned on for several years, alternately dying away to a whisper and then flickering back into public attention. Time and usage have a way of making the ungainly appear to be less graceless. So it was with the national name. Despite its shortcomings, United States of America had become entrenched, habitual, accepted. The nation had its final place-name—awkward, unwieldy, impersonal and geographically inexact though it may be. Any who persist today in retaining lingering doubts about the name may perhaps find some comfort in the fact that the nation's chief rival on the world stage has a name even more cumbersome and cold: the Union of Soviet Socialist Republics.

4

The Stately Procession

If there had been numerous twists and turns en route to the national name, the road to the state names was even more of a corkscrew. After all, that road had to reach fifty different destinations.

Naming the thirteen original states was so simple a matter it gave no hint of what would come later; it required only the substitution of "state" for "colony" in the titles they already bore. Eight of those names had been created as tributes to English aristocracy. Sir Walter Raleigh, the man with the most famous cape in history, coined "Virginia" in 1584 to honor Queen Elizabeth, the Virgin Queen. (When a group of Virginians broke away 277 years later to found the new state of West Virginia, Sir Walter's tribute became extended further.)

A successor to Elizabeth's throne, Charles I, did not wait for a Sir Walter to come along—in 1629 he honored himself when he made a grant of American land by naming it Carolana from Carolus, the latin form of Charles. The spelling was later altered to Carolina and then—because the grant was too large to administer effectively as a single unit—in 1690 it was split into North Carolina and South Carolina, so Charles I, like Elizabeth, the Virgin Queen, ended up being twice honored. To please his wife, Queen Henrietta Maria, Charles I conferred linguistic immortality on her in 1632 by concocting *Terra Mariae*—Maria's Land—as the name of a new American colony; in the actual charter delivered to Lord Baltimore the Latin name was written in its English form, Maryland.

The Duke of York and Albany, son of Charles I, was bitten by the same place-name bug as his parents, and Colonel Richard Nicolls was aware of it. Sent to America by the Duke to command English troops ousting the Dutch from their colonial land holdings, Nicolls proceeded to butter up his aristocratic sponsor by renaming both the Dutch colony and its chief city to New York in his honor. He spread the butter thicker by also renaming the colony's other major city from Beverwyck to Albany. The Duke of York and Albany was also the source of another state name. To escape enemies plotting against him in the mid-1600s he had taken refuge for a time with Sir George Carteret, governor of the English island of Jersey. In gratitude, the Duke cut off a portion of the New York colony in 1664 and regranted it to Sir George and his friend Lord Berkeley, at the same time naming it New Jersey to commemorate his place of refuge. Thus, five states trace their names to the Duke and his parents.

South of this rash of father-wife-son place-names James Oglethorpe coined "Georgia" in 1732 in honor of George II. Next door to Henrietta Maria's Maryland, Delaware borrowed its name from Lord De La Ware. The remaining five of the original thirteen state names are a mixed bag.

Both Connecticut and Massachusetts are Indian in origin. Connecticut is the modified form of Quinatucquet, "upon the long river." The Indians had applied Quinatucquet only to the tidal basin at the mouth of the river but British seamen exploring the area mistakenly assumed it covered the river as a whole and they labeled the river that way on their maps. Later, the name that began in error was extended to the land surrounding the river.

Massachusetts is derived from the name of a tribe that lived in the area around Boston. The colonists would probably have done better to have chosen Wampanoag as their place-name since the Massachusetts were a small, dying tribe as a result of a plague suffered a few years earlier, while the Wampanoags were the dominant tribe in the region. Furthermore, it was Massasoit— the intelligent, benevolent chief of the Wampanoags—who taught the white settlers how to adapt to the land and how to cope with the often harsh realities of its nature.

When William Penn received his grant of land in America in 1681, he notified the English Privy Council that he wished to call it New Wales out of respect for his Welsh ancestors. The Council rejected his proposal, so Penn went back to the drawing board and created Sylvania from the Latin *sylvanus*—forest—because of the extensive woodlands carpeting his grant. The Privy Council accepted the new name, but King Charles II tacked Penn in front of it to show his regard for Penn's father, Admiral William Penn. The king also had another reason for the addition—he thought it might make the admiral happier about the grant since it was being made to the son to wipe out most of a large sum of money owed to the father.

The selection of New Hampshire was a simple, straightforward matter. Captain John Mason, the grant holder, chose that name because of his fond recollections of the English county of Hampshire where he had lived before embarking for America.

Even today there is disagreement over the origin of Rhode Island's name. One theory traces it back to an account in 1524 by Giovanni da Verrazano, the Italian mariner, in which he described the island which constitutes much of the present state as resembling the Isle of Rhodes in the Aegean Sea near Turkey. It is a plausible explanation because Verrazano was in fact familiar with the Aegean lands and it is possible to note some similarity between Rhode Island and Rhodes.

But the second theory, which is the one most widely believed, is that Adrian Block, a Dutch navigator mapping the region a century after Verrazano, conceived the name Roodt Eylandt, Dutch for "red island," because of the red clay he observed on the shore, and the English—who made a habit of squeezing Dutch names into English molds—later Anglicized it into Rhode Island. In any event, regardless of which theory may be correct, Rhode Island is not the proper legal name of the state. Officially it is Rhode Island and Providence Plantations, thus giving to the smallest of the states the longest of the names. In 1776 that elongated title was adopted as a way to commemorate the colony's first white settlement, Providence Plantations.

Although eight of the original thirteen states had been named in tribute to ranking personages, of the thirty-seven states that followed that initial thirteen into the Union only two—Louisiana and Washington—carried designations created to honor individuals. The explorer La Salle coined "Louisiana" in 1682—writing it La Louisianne—in tribute to his king, Louis XIV of France. Washington, adopted to honor George Washington (after squelching those who thought that Columbia would be a better choice), is the sole state name that pays homage to an American.

Like Connecticut of the original thirteen, seven of the later state names—Colorado, Minnesota, Mississippi, Nebraska, Ohio, Oregon and Wisconsin—originated as purely river names. Their transition from designation for a river to designation for a state was seldom smooth, direct, or free of confusion. The case of Colorado illustrates the point.

In 1859 Congress began consideration of a proposal to grant territorial status to a western region as a prelude to its statehood. The matter was debated over an extended period of time in the House and the Senate committees responsible for territorial affairs, and in both committees a major stumbling block was what to name the new territory. The House debated the relative merits of Colona, Osage, Lafayette, and Franklin, and usually the debate was quite heated. Debate in the Senate committee was no less heated and revolved around an entirely different set of proposed names: Yampa, Idaho, San Juan, Arapahoe, and Colorado. Nobody was willing to concede that someone else's favorite had more merit than his own, so a deadlock persisted for two years.

Finally, in 1861, the Senate Committee on Territories decided to recommend to the full Senate that it select Idaho. When the bill was introduced on the floor of the Senate the partisans of Colorado made one ultimate, heroic effort to have their way, offering an amendment to strike Idaho from the bill and in its place to insert Colorado as the name of the new territory. With flowery eloquence they argued that Colorado was a lovely name, rhythmic, melodious, and with a rich historic heritage. Warming to their task, they traced the path of Juan de Oñate who pressed northwest from Mexico in 1598 seeking gold for the Mexican viceroy. Oñate found no gold, they said, but discovered something of equal value—a river whose waters had a lustrous reddish hue, the result of its mineral and vegetable content combined with the sunlight dappling its surface, and he named it the Colorado, Spanish for "red-hued." How, they asked, could the Senate fail to be moved by a name of such magnificence and such historic proportions?

Weary of the whole matter, the Senate approved the amended bill. The House, equally weary, went along with the Senate even though Colorado had not been among the names they had argued over for the last two years. But Congress was not yet finished with the matter. In 1876, in elevating Colorado from a territory to a state, Congress realigned its borders, cutting off the western portion containing the headwaters of the Colorado River and leaving within the redrawn state only a tributary called the Grand River. This created the paradox of a state that was named for a river except that the river no longer flowed in the state to which it had given its name. To erase the problem it had created, in

1921 Congress adopted legislation changing the name of the Grand River to the Colorado River.

Ten state names—Alabama, Arkansas, Idaho, Illinois, Iowa, Kansas, Missouri, North Dakota, South Dakota, and Utah—are derived from Indian tribal names. Two more—Indiana and Oklahoma—can be included in this category although, strictly speaking, they are not really tribal names. Indiana was conceived as a state name referring to Indian tribes generally rather than to a specific tribe. Oklahoma was coined in 1866 by the Reverend Allen White, a Christianized Choctaw missionary, from two Choctaw words—*ukla,* meaning "person," and *huma,* meaning "red"—as a reference to the red man generally.

Tribal names did not become state names any more gracefully or smoothly than did river names. For instance, early French explorers and fur traders reported frequent encounters with a tribe whose name they recorded with dozens of different spellings according to who was doing the writing. That tribal region passed to the jurisdiction of the United States when it was included in the vast lands transferred by the French to the Americans under terms of the Lousiana Purchase of 1803. One French version of the tribal name—Kansas—was applied by Congress to a state it carved from a part of those lands. But Congress also used another French version of the same tribal name—Arkansas— for a second state it created in another section of the lands. This was confusing enough, but there was more to come.

There are two ways to pronounce Arkansas—either with the final *s* silent in the French manner, as though it were spelled "Arkansaw," or with the final *s* pronounced as in the case of Kansas—and Congress itself had difficulty in deciding which pronunciation it favored. In legislation it adopted in 1819, Congress leaned toward "Arkansaw" and to make its feelings clear adopted Arkansaw as the official spelling. But in 1836, when it granted statehood, Congress reversed itself and altered the official name to Arkansas. All that Congress had accomplished by its change of heart was to perpetuate the two conflicting pronunciations. To try to settle matters once and for all, the Arkansas legislature in 1881 adopted a bill proclaiming the official pronunciation to be Arkansas with the final *s* silent, as though the name were actually Arkansaw. Of course, it is obvious that Arkansas and Kansas cannot both be an accurate rendition of the same tribal name. It appears that both are wrong; according to a Smithsonian Institution report issued in 1954, the proper tribal name was probably Kánze.

Of the fifteen state names thus far not accounted for, twelve—Alaska, Arizona, California, Hawaii, Kentucky, Maine, Michigan, Nevada, New Mexico, Tennessee, Vermont and Wyoming—had already existed as place-names before their meanings were extended to embrace the states they came to designate. In many ways they are the most curious of the state names. Like Tennessee which—in its original form of Tanasi—was the place-name of not one, but of two different Cherokee villages. Or Arizona which—before it was extended to the state and before the Spanish corrupted it from the original Arishóonak—simply identified springs that are not even within the present state but are located in northern Mexico. Or Hawaii, "homeland," applied by the natives to only one of their eight major islands but later broadened to designate them all collectively, replacing the name the English had bestowed—the Sandwich Islands (for the same Earl of Sandwich who discovered that meat tasted as good between two slices of bread as on a plate).

Oddly enough, three widely separated, completely dissimilar states—Michigan, Kentucky and Wyoming—created their names from existing place-names that each had been formed from a different tribal language, yet each has an almost identical meaning. Michigan—from the Chippewa *Majiigan*—means "clearing" and originally it designated a large, flat, cleared section within the present state. Kentucky is a Wyandot word meaning "plain." Initially it applied only to a stretch of prairie land in the central portion of the state.

"Wyoming," which sounds so thoroughly western that you involuntarily look around for the sagebrush and tumbleweeds when you hear it spoken, is about as eastern as it can be without winding up in the Atlantic Ocean. Emerging from an eastern tribal dialect, Wyoming means "large plains" and for a long time it referred only to a broad, shallow valley in Pennsylvania. In 1778 white settlers in Pennsylvania's Wyoming Valley were slain by Indians in a massacre that aroused the whole country and made the name almost a household word. The familiarity of the name was later reinforced when Thomas Campbell's epic poem about the massacre, *Gertrude of Wyoming,* captured popular imagination. Congress, stimulated by the spirited urging of Pennsylvania legislators anxious to see one of their place-names elevated to new importance, adopted the thoroughly familiar eastern name for the western region it organized into a territory in 1868.

Another similarity of meaning links two other widely separated states whose names were enlarged from existing place-names. Alaska—from an Aleut word meaning "mainland"—was used by the Aleuts to designate the continental portion of their region to distinguish it from the long chain of islands that stretch out from the coast. Maine's early colonists referred to their continental area as "the main"—short for "mainland"—to set it apart from their hundreds of off-shore islands. Even today, old-time Maine islanders still often say they are "going to the main" when they set out for the mainland. (A rival opinion persists that Maine may in fact have been named for the Maine which at one time had been a province of France, but this does not seem to be a very likely theory.)

Vermont traces its origin back to 1647 when the French explorer, Samuel de Champlain, wrote Verd Mont—"green mountain"—on his map to designate the high, forested ridges he observed. New Mexico and Nevada are of Spanish coinage. The rulers of Mexico—which itself had been adopted by the Spanish from an old Aztec place-name meaning "place of the Aztec god, Mexìtli"—designated the upper Rio Grande region of their domain as Nuevo México; when it was annexed to the United

States in 1846, its designation was retained but was Anglicized to New Mexico.

Nevada is in reality only half of an earlier place-name. As far back as the seventeenth century Spanish mariners sailing off the west coast of the continent had referred to the snow covered mountains they glimpsed as the Sierra Nevada, the "snowy range." In 1858, when Congress voted to carve a new territory out of the western portion of Utah, the legislators decided, somewhat quirkily, to give it half of the Spanish place-name. In any event, the congressmen were a bit soft on their geography because very little of the Sierra Nevada is actually in Nevada; most of the mountain range is in California.

Of all of the states whose names emerged from existing place-names, California's case is perhaps the most curious. The name appear first in a Spanish romantic novel—*Las Sergas de Esplandián*—written by Garcia Ordóñez de Montalvo in 1510. In his popular novel Montalvo described a mythical island "on the right hand of the Indies" that he dubbed California. When the Spanish explorer Hernando Cortés probed the Pacific coast and discovered what he supposed to be an island "on the right hand of the Indies" he was struck by the similiarity to Montalvo's California, so he gave that fictional place-name to his discovery. Later exploration revealed that Cortés' island was in fact a peninsula rather than an island but the name stuck and crept up the coast from the peninsula of Lower California to extend to the region that eventually became the thirty-first state.

Since Florida's creation as a place-name by Ponce de León in 1513 has already been recounted, only two in the stately procession remain to be accounted for: Montana and Texas.

Montana, Latin for "mountainous," existed for a time as the name of a small town that flourished briefly and then expired without a whimper in the Pike's Peak goldfields of the late 1850s. It is possible that Congressman James M. Ashley of Ohio passed through the short-lived town when he had been a footloose vagabond roaming the west in his precongressional days. Maybe he had been attracted by the place-name's brevity and its suitability to the rugged nature of that section of the country. Whatever the source of his inspiration, he strongly urged his fellow congressmen in 1863 to give the name of Montana to a new territory they were then in the process of organizing in a mountainous western region. Ashley was disappointed when his colleagues, spurning his proposal, named the territory for a local Indian tribe, the Idaho.

From the very outset there was bickering between inhabitants of eastern Idaho and those of western Idaho. Within one year the easterners petitioned Congress to cut them away from the rest of Idaho and organize them as a separate territory of their own. Congress was agreeable. A persistent man and one who did not shrug off rebuffs lightly, Ashley again urged adoption of Montana as the place-name when Congress got down to the business of creating the new territory. Again the response from his colleagues was lukewarm at best.

But this time Ashley dug in his heels and refused to be budged from his obstinate insistence that Montana be approved. His obstinacy was prompted only in part by his fondness for the name; he also held firm to Montana because he was deadset against the name being actively considered for adoption: Jefferson. Thomas Jefferson had planted the seed that had blossomed into the Democratic Party, and Ashley, a staunch Republican, was determined to prevent the nation's first Democrat from being memorialized in the roll call of the states. With dogged persistence he chipped away at the pro-Jefferson bloc while at the same time he hammered together a coalition to push for Montana. In the end Ashley managed to engineer a vote in favor of his place-name candidate.

Last, but far from least, is the biggest state, Texas. Early Spanish explorers probing a region in the southwest occupied by tribes of the Caddo confederacy heard Indians throughout the area use one word repeatedly. The explorers recorded it in their reports sometimes as "Texas," sometimes as "Tejas," sometimes in other though similar forms. In the beginning the Spanish assumed the word to be the name by which the Caddos designated themselves or their land or both. Soon, however, they discovered the word was actually a peaceful Caddo greeting that can best be translated as "Hello, friend." Growing accustomed to the word that was repeated so frequently, the Spanish fell into the habit of referring to the Caddo land as El Reino de los Texas, "The Kingdom of Texas."

Texas became an actual place-name in 1690 when the Spanish built a mission settlement among the Caddos and called it San Francisco de los Texas. However, it was not as an extension of the mission name but as an outgrowth of the universal Caddo greeting that Texas came to be the official designation for the region. The name remained attached to the republic that was eventually created and to the state into which the republic evolved.

The naming of the fifty states shows what a varied nation this is. What had commenced largely as an exercise in selecting names to honor and flatter the nobility had developed into something quite different by the time all fifty states had received their names. Along the way it transformed rivers and tribes and mountains, an Aztec god and a fictional island, a friendly greeting and a religious day, and various other things, into state names. It had dipped into a score of different languages and dialects to withdraw words and rearrange them into patterns that altered their shapes. It had aroused passions and provoked intrigues. Most of all, it had been a spirited, lively process suited to a spirited, lively country.

5

The Place-Name Explosion

Place-naming in America had been bubbling along vigorously for the three centuries since Ponce de León had created Florida as the designation for his landfall in the south, but in the 1800s the pot boiled over in a huge spray of new names.

The young nation was flexing its muscles, stretching, reaching, extending itself. Its rapidly growing population spread over the beckoning continent. In stagecoaches, in long, lumbering wagon trains, on horseback people surged in all directions. On paddle-wheel riverboat, on mule-drawn barge, on log rafts; in gritty, dusty cars jouncing and swaying behind smoke-belching engines grinding along fresh-laid rails that were beginning to staple one section of the country to the next. Young America was on the move seeking new lands, new fortunes, new adventures. Wherever people stopped—either to sink roots or merely to rest for a while before moving on again—they added fresh names to the rapidly changing map of the nation.

The Revolutionary War had brought more than political independence to America—it had brought independence of spirit and of individual attitude. The American who emerged from the war was a product of his past, but no longer chained to it. He had been liberated by his New World environment and experiences and by the democratic philosophy of the newly created nation. Now he had his own notions about everything, including how to name the places he was building. So he named uninhibitedly, unchecked—with zest instead of system.

There was no consistency, no uniformity, to the names being created to fill in the blank spaces on the map. Nationhood had come too recently and political matters loomed too urgently for the federal authorities to turn their attention to the way in which the country's geography was being labeled. In the absence of a national system to establish standards and regulate procedures place-naming was often a matter of chance, of local whim, of spur-of-the-moment decision reflecting the thoughts and attitudes of the creators at the moment of creation. Because the creators were so varied in background and character, because they sought different goals, the names they coined were similarly varied. The names ranged from homespun and unassuming to pompous and pretentious, from familiar to freakish, from serious to comic, from bland to colorful, from well-mannered to impudent.

But if there was no strong, central thread weaving the flood of place-names together in a single grand design, there were patterns of similarity. There were, for instance, the names erected as monuments to those who found special favor in the eyes of the namers. Chief among those honored in this way were the heroes of the Revolution—Washington in scores of places including, fittingly, the nation's capital, Jefferson, Hancock, Franklin, Revere, Madison, Adams, Knox, Hamilton. Nor were the foreign volunteers who had contributed their skill and courage to the Revolution, and sometimes their lives, forgotten by the place-namers—Pulaski, von Steuben, Kosciusko, De Kalb, De Grasse, and especially Lafayette.

So many places styled themselves Lafayette that the postal

authorities cried out, "Enough!" The great number of Lafayettes created confusion, causing mail to be delivered to the wrong place. Many place-names resourcefully proceeded to outwit the postal officials by creating such variations as Lafayette Hill, Lafayette Springs, Fayette, Fayette City, and Fayetteville. A number of towns even devised a way to honor the Frenchman without using his name at all: they simply styled themselves La Grange after his estate in France.

Not only heroes were being immortalized on the developing map of America. Ordinary citizens, sometimes even disreputable people, were honored with place-names.

The founders of a community in Kansas played poker to determine who would name the town; the winner, E. H. Cawker, christened it Cawker City in honor of himself. The Louisiana town that developed in what had formerly been a hideaway for pirates named itself Lafitte for Jean Lafitte, the most notorious pirate who had taken refuge there.

The three founders of a settlement in Illinois decided it was only fair that the place be named for them. This was easy since the trio—Shultz, Schroth, and Willi—shared the same first name of Jacob. But they really glorified themselves when they dubbed the town Saint Jacob.

Laramie, Wyoming, is a linguistic memorial to a hard-bitten, crusty fur trapper, Jacques La Ramie. D. W. Alderman, founder of a South Carolina town, created its name in honor of himself and two families of his relatives—the Colemans and the Lulas—by taking the first two letters from each last name to form "Alcolu." And in 1820 a Maryland town named itself Frostburg for its local tavern keeper, Meshack Frost.

Of everyone memorialized by place-names, the largest single group consisted of individuals associated with railroads. Under the circumstances, it was almost unavoidable. The rails were pushing out through sparsely settled country, and, to create customers for their services, rail companies were busily laying out town sites along their tracks. Even where the companies did not actually sponsor the towns their rails served as magnets for settlement, and communities grew up around junction points, freight depots, and repair yards. Thus, in hundreds of new communities the railroad was by far the dominant force controlling local affairs.

One of the ways the railroads exercised their power was to cater to the vanity of their officials by naming towns after them. Dillon, Montana, was named for Sidney Dillon, president of the Union Pacific. The president of a competing railroad in Montana, the Northern Pacific, made Dillon seem like a piker: Frederick Billings had a whole county named for him, while a Northern Pacific freight depot that became Montana's largest city was named Billings for his son, Parmley. I. T. Burr, vice-president of the Atchison, Topeka and Santa Fe, achieved his measure of immortality when Burrton, Kansas, was named for him.

Another Kansas town, Ellinwood, was named for a Santa Fe engineer. Salamanca, New York, was named for a major stockholder of the Atlantic and Great Western. Goodman, Mississippi, styled itself after the president of the Mississippi Central; Rhinelander, Wisconsin, after the president of the Milwaukee, Lake Shore and Western; and Burt, Iowa, after an executive of the Union Pacific. A vice-president of the Kansas City, Memphis and Birmingham Railroad named Nettleton had two towns named for him, one in Mississippi and the other in Missouri. George W. Cass, a director of the Northern Pacific, had both a county and a town in North Dakota named for him.

This matter of titling places for railroad figures did not always run true to form. A rail executive in Iowa named a town Colo after his pet dog; there may have been some justice in this since a short time earlier Colo had been struck and killed by a train. In South Carolina, a railroad official, hoping to win over a local lady he was smitten with, named her community Ora after her; the records do not reveal whether his action gained him his prize.

In the state of Washington a railroad official named a town

Ralston after his favorite breakfast cereal. But in California when executives of the Central Pacific decided to christen a community Ralston—to flatter W. C. Ralston, an influential San Francisco banker whose support they wanted—the banker declared he was too unimportant for such recognition and he declined the honor. The executives, to whom such modesty was a source of amazement, named the town Modesto instead.

In Arkansas, when the Kansas City Southern found itself in financial difficulties, a wealthy Dutchman came to the rescue with a large, timely investment in the company; as a mark of gratitude, the railroad invited the investor to name a town on its trackage. Unlike the San Francisco banker, the Dutchman was not a modest soul; he named the town "De Geoijin" after himself. The trouble was that nobody in the place could spell or pronounce De Geoijin properly. To solve the problem the railroad and the residents entered into a quiet little conspiracy whereby they altered it to the more manageable De Queen.

One large grouping of nineteenth-century names has a familiar ring. These are the repeaters, place-names already established elsewhere and transplanted to fresh surroundings. Many who migrated to new locations felt a need to soften the harsh strangeness of their surroundings, to preserve a reassuring link with the old and the familiar, by importing their home town names. Who can fail to recognize the New England origins of the Ohio pioneers who founded such Buckeye State cities as Amherst, Bridgeport, Cambridge, Greenwich, Hartford, New Boston, and Portsmouth? Syracuse, Kansas, was established by New York Syracusans; New London, Wisconsin, by Connecticut New Londoners; Oswego, Montana, by New York Oswegans; Lancaster, South Carolina, by settlers from Lancaster, Pennsylvania; and Richmond in a half-dozen states by settlers from Richmond, Virginia. On the other hand, Lisbon, North Dakota, was a single blossom from a double transplantation. It was named by two of its founders for their separate hometowns—Lisbon, Illinois, and Lisbon, New York.

Sometimes established place-names were transplanted and re-transplanted. A group from Rutland, Massachusetts, journeyed north to Vermont where they founded a town they called Rutland after their old home. A later generation, restless like their fathers before them, set out from Rutland, Vermont, to Illinois where they established a new Rutland named for their Vermont home. Of course, even the original Rutland in Massachusetts was itself a transplantation, having been brought to America by immigrants from Rutland, England.

Many of the repeaters originated abroad. Some had been imported by immigrants, but a great number were chosen by native-born place-namers either because they admired the city whose name they were borrowing or because they hoped some of the importance and affluence of that city would rub off on their communities along with the name. Whatever the reason, hundreds of nineteenth-century American towns styled themselves Versailles, Rome, Vienna, Warsaw, Brussels, Hamburg, Antwerp, Amsterdam, Naples, Madrid, Dublin, London, Liverpool, Melbourne, Glasgow, Cairo, and all the rest. Few important foreign cities, especially those in Europe, escaped transplantation to America although sometimes a Yankee tail was tied to them—like Berlin Center, Berlin Heights, and Geneva-on-the-Lake, Ohio; Paris Station, and Venice Center, New York; Moscow Mills, Missouri; and Belgrade Lakes, Maine.

Another large grouping of place-names was created with a pair of scissors by geography-minded names. They flourished in communities on or near state lines. The christeners snipped a piece from the name of each state and pasted the pieces together to create a name for the community. Scissor-wielding created "Monida," which is in Montana within spitting distance of Idaho. On the line separating Delaware and Maryland is the town of Delmar; farther north on the same state line is the town of Marydel. Texhoma is located where Texas and Oklahoma rub elbows, Tennga where Tennessee and Georgia meet, Kanorada where Kansas and Colorado meet, Kenvir where Kentucky nestles against Virginia, and Michiaha where Michigan joins Indiana.

Scissor-wielding place-namers cut some of their fanciest snippets in towns established near the junction of more than two states. If you get an itch in Kenova you can scratch it in Kentucky, Ohio, or West Virginia. And Texarkana is located near the junction of Texas, Arkansas, and Louisiana. Place-naming via a pair of scissors even became international—Calexico is located in California just north of the Mexican border; its twin city just south of the border is Mexicali.

One sizable group of place-namers consisted of the culture conscious. Because their new, little towns were so raw and unfinished, so lacking in any real cultural life, they tried to bring at least a hint of intellectual refinement and elegance to their communities by turning to literature for inspiration for their place-names. Ovid, New York, was named after an eminent poet of ancient Rome. (But Ovid, Michigan, was not inspired by culture; it acquired its name by transplantation of settlers from Ovid, New York.)

Milton, Vermont, was named for the English poet John Milton, and Sidney, Ohio, for another English poet, Sir Philip Sidney. Elsinore, Utah, was named for the setting of Shakespeare's *Hamlet;* Othello, Washington, for Shakespeare's classic tragedy; Hugo, Oklahoma, for the French novelist Victor Hugo; Lake Ibsen, North Dakota, for the Norwegian dramatist Henrik Ibsen; Dante, South Dakota, for the Italian poet Dante Alighieri; and Auburn, New York, for the Irish village that is the scene of Oliver Goldsmith's poem *The Deserted Village.*

Plato, Missouri, was named for the Greek philosopher, and towns in a dozen states were dubbed Athens for the Greek city that was the cultural center of the ancient world. Rudyard Kipling was cut down the middle in Michigan where one town became Rudyard and the second became Kipling. In California, instead of making two out of one, one was made out of two when Mark Twain was grafted to Bret Harte to become the town of Twain Harte.

In Indiana the man who would later become ninth President of the United States—William Henry Harrison—hummed a tune as he made plans for a town to be established on a tract of land he owned. He hummed that composition often because it was his favorite—"Pastoral Elegy." Inspired by the composition, Harrison named the town Corydon after the shepherd in the song's lyrics.

Meanwhile, over in Minnesota, the founders of a community named it Ivanhoe after Sir Walter Scott's famous novel, and then named the streets for characters in the novel.

Some other Minnesotans turned to the American poet Henry Wadsworth Longfellow for their place-name. From Longfellow's *The Song of Hiawatha,* they chose Minnehaha, the Indian heroine. Then they added *polis*—Greek for "city"—to the end to coin "Minnehahapolis." They soon agreed that they had bitten off a little more than they wanted to chew so they shortened the cumbersome Minnehahapolis into the less unwieldy Minneapolis.

While names were used by some to try to spray an aura of culture over their communities, others turned to religion to seek a place-name atmosphere of purity and spirituality. From the Bible came the stimulation for such place-names as Bethlehem, Nazareth, Moab, Jerusalem, Jericho, Hebron, Samaria, Gilead, Galilee, Bethany, Bethel, and Ephraim. A town in Illinois became Bible Grove and one in New York became Bible School Park. A California town became Holy City and one in Montana became Pray. Hawaiian Mormons who settled in Utah named their village Iosepa—Hawaiian for Joseph—in honor of Joseph Smith, the father of Mormonism. Church-minded Kansans christened their town "Sabetha," deriving the designation from the Biblical injunction to observe the Sabbath as a holy day. And the founders of a Minnesota community named it Jericho for the Biblical river, then opened a municipally owned saloon whose profits financed the public budget.

One enduring scrap in the patchwork quilt of American place-names was stitched by those whose gaze was fixed firmly on the surrounding land and its natural life. Thus emerged such Mississippi towns as Alligator, Blue Mountain, Duck Hill, Hickory Flat, Magnolia, Mineral Springs, Moss Point, Olive Branch, Panther Burn, Piney Woods, Swan Lake, Walnut, and Water Valley.

Similiar place-name naturalists were responsible for such Virginia towns as Acorn, Bee, Birdsnest, Clover, Cuckoo, Hyacinth, Meadows of Dan, Natural Bridge, Orchid, Oyster and Rockfish. They coined Bivalve, Chestnut, Cranberry Lake, and Maple Shade in New Jersey; Beaver, Broad Bottom, Butterfly, Crane Nest, Frozen Lake, Pigeonroost, Sassafras, Soft Shell, and Turkey in Kentucky; Antelope, Cottonwood Falls, Gypsum, Pretty Prairie, Shallow Water, and Sunflower in Kansas; and Cherrylog, Dewy Rose, Flowery Branch, High Shoals, Locust Grove, and Rising Fawn in Georgia.

Then there were the bait place-namers who turned out linguistic lures in much the same way as a fisherman ties a hula popper and a shiny spinner to the end of his line. The bait names had one purpose—to create an image that potential settlers would find so irresistibly attractive that they would become hooked on the community and could be reeled in. Usually the bait names were created by companies that had bought a large chunk of land, had laid it out as a town, and now were trying their energetic best to sell off the lots. The enticing names they devised held out promises that the raw sites were seldom in a position to deliver—names like Prosperity, Grandview, Pleasantville, Paradise, Richlands, Sunnyside, Good Hope, and Sweetwater—nevertheless, they did hook a lot of fish and eventually many of the promises even came true, given enough sweating and straining by those who had been snagged.

The bait-namers were shrewd practitioners of their craft, able to design their lures in such a way that it would attract a specific fish. The Maine legislature, concerned because the Pine Tree State's 33,000 square miles were so sparsely populated, commissioned William W. Thomas in 1870 to seek out settlers.

Thomas had previously served as United States diplomatic representative to Sweden and he concluded that his best bet was to concentrate on his contacts in that country. He selected one of the most underpopulated sites in Maine, baited it with Sweden as its place-name, and then sailed abroad to dangle Maine's Sweden in front of the Swedes. He returned with fifty immigrants. Thomas selected a second Maine site, baited it with the place-name of Stockholm, and lured another contingent of Swedes to settle there.

But when all is said and done, one group of place-names stands out from all the rest as distinctively, unmistakably American. What links these names together and sets them apart from the others is the way they reflect the crudeness, rambunctiousness, hazards, and earthy humor of nineteenth-century frontier life. These are names that never beat about the bush, never pussy-footed. They were a forthright product of their times.

You can almost smell the gun oil and harness leather, almost feel the mud sucking at your boots in wet weather, and the dust gritty against your skin in dry, almost see the cocky swagger, almost hear the clink of poker chips or the echoes of rowdy laughter in place-names like Hell's Half Acre, Chugwater, and Saddlestring, Wyoming; Rough And Ready, Whiskeytown, and Fiddletown, California; Braggadocio, Faro, Hurricane Deck, and Black Jack, Missouri; Wild Horse and Rifle, Colorado. Names like Cut And Shoot, Muleshoe, and Spur, Texas; Skull Valley, Tombstone, Happy Jack, and Maverick, Arizona; Hungry Horse and Roundup, Montana; Rawhide, Nevada; Mustang, Oklahoma; Joker, West Virginia; Tomahawk, Kentucky; Dutch John, Utah; Mud Butte, South Dakota; Cayuse, Oregon. These are names that are pungent and spicy on the tongue, full-flavored, peppery, hearty names to bite into, not to nibble around.

In one way or another, America was getting her place-names. A bountiful, exuberant outpouring of names. A profusion of names. A confusion of names.

6

A President Takes a Hand

By the time the United States reached its one hundredth birthday as a sovereign nation it was paying a high price for its failure to establish rational, sensible controls over the place-naming process. The long period of rapid expansion and town-building had flooded the land with names that were bogging it down. Freight, mail, and people wound up in the wrong places with maddening frequency, led astray by place-names that closely resembled one another or that were actually carbon copies of each other.

Irwinton, Alabama, and Irwinton in neighboring Georgia were continually victimized by their identical names. In 1843, after he missed out on an important business transaction because the documents he was awaiting were delivered to the wrong Irwinton, the leading banker in the Alabama Irwinton lost his patience and arbitrarily changed his town's name to Eufala, deriving it from an Indian word meaning "beech tree."

Mount Tabor, North Carolina, and Mount Tabor, South

Carolina were hamstrung because they were constantly being confused with one another. In desperation, the Mount Tabor in South Carolina dropped the "Mount" from its title and spelled Tabor backwards to become Robat.

The woes of Irwinton and Mount Tabor were repeated daily in hundreds of other places across the country. Small wonder— there were a score of Alexandrias, Washingtons, Franklins, Troys, Princetons, Manchesters, Greenvilles, Newports, Chesters, Arlingtons, and Marions. There were some fifty versions of Cedar. Some seventy-five towns were styled Summit. Nearly twenty states had more than one Summit within their borders; four states had at least four Summits each. Even an offbeat place-name like Chili was repeated numerous times; one state —New York—had a Chili, a North Chili, and a South Chili. In Indiana, two towns only fifty miles from one another were named Scipio. (The two Scipios are still there, still confounding and confusing the unwary.)

Place-name entanglements were tripping up government bureaus, business houses, shipping firms, industrial enterprises, editors, educators, and just plain citizens. The situation was bad, and getting worse, when Thomas C. Mendenhall decided to do something about it. Mendenhall was in a good position to try to save the nation from falling over its place-names.

Serving as superintendent of the U.S. Coast and Geodetic Survey, Dr. Mendenhall was acutely sensitive to the place-name mess because he worked with the names daily in carrying out the functions of his office. He assumed that "all who have engaged at any time in the preparation of maps, charts, gazetteers, or any other documents of a geographical nature" must be as frustrated by the confusion as he, and he also assumed that as professional geographers they would be willing to join him in trying to shape a solution.

On January 8, 1890, Mendenhall invited the director of the U.S. Geological Survey, the commissioner of the General Land Office, the Army Chief of Engineers, the hydrographer of the

Navy, the postmaster general, the chairman of the Lighthouse Board, and the president of the National Geographic Society to designate a suitable member of their respective staffs to meet with him informally to consider the problem. All responded favorably, naming representatives. A short time later a State Department delegate was added to the membership of the Mendenhall committee.

The group met regularly through the spring and summer of 1890 to analyze the situation. The picture that emerged from their deliberations was even more confused than they had imagined. They found that their own agencies had created at least as much of the chaos as had the sustained wave of local, do-it-yourself place-naming. The several federal agencies involved in compiling maps and geographic data were, they learned, consistently inconsistent in their use of place-names. A map compiled by one department would label a place with one name while a map produced by a second department would use a different name—or the same name spelled differently—for the same place, but still another map produced by still another federal bureau would employ still another name for the identical place. The committee found that even within a single department place-names would differ from map to map and from document to document.

In those freewheeling days it even was quite common for a place to go under more than one name. To begin with, a town would have the title officially adopted for it by the municipal authorities. But its post office might, and frequently did, have another name designated for it by the Post Office Department, while its railroad station often had still a different name bestowed on it by the railroad serving the town. If there were a local military installation or a lighthouse, the departments responsible for them might list their location under place-names unique to them alone. In addition, if the town served as a county seat the county authorities often—especially in the South—had their own designation for the community.

Raleigh County authorities, for example, designated Beckley, West Virginia, as Raleigh Court House despite the fact that the municipal authorities insisted it was Beckley. To muddy the murky waters further, the residents of a town might stubbornly persist in calling it by an old, informal name that had been in vogue before the town fathers got around to adopting an official designation.

The upshot was that if you asked what a place was called you might well end up with different answers from the mailman, the railroad conductor, the mayor, the county commissioner, the soldier, the lighthouse keeper, the mapmaker, and the residents themselves. Even if there happened to be a measure of agreement on the name, there was often disagreement on how it ought to be spelled. Like Mrs. Murphy's chowder, place-names bubbled in a steaming caldron that had many strange ingredients tossed into it.

The Mendenhall committee could take no direct action to improve the recipe for the chowder because it was an informal body powerless to issue official directives. So it did the next best thing by writing a comprehensive report of its findings and sending it to the White House. Disturbed by the revelations contained in the report, on September 4, 1890, President Benjamin Harrison issued an executive order establishing the United States Board on Geographic Names to bring order out of the chaos. President Harrison named ten men, with Dr. Mendenhall as chairman, to serve on the board.

At long last the nation had taken its first step on the march toward a rational system of naming places. It was, however, a mincing, waltzing step instead of a firm tread. For one thing President Harrison failed to authorize either a staff or a budget for the board, specifying that the Board on Geographic Names (BGN) "shall entail no expense on the Government." For another thing, each of the ten appointed to the BGN were already employees of other federal departments and Harrison directed that they would continue in their full-time jobs while serving on the board part-time "without additional compensation."

There was a third flaw in the establishment of the BGN: its decisions were to be binding only on federal departments. Local jurisdictions and private agencies were to be free to accept or to reject BGN decisions as they saw fit. This had the potential to make the board's work completely meaningless, but it turned out to be a much less grave shortcoming than it seemed initially. As a practical matter, in the face of the mandatory acceptance of BGN decisions by all federal agencies it was difficult for othes to resist falling into line. A would-be holdout very soon discovered that it was very lonely being the only one rallying around a place-name that was ignored on all federal maps, in all federal correspondence, and by the post office.

In its first year of operation the board tackled two different tasks. First, it drew up a list of principles that set forth rules for the form and spelling of place-names. Second, it considered 2,000 cases in which places were identified by more than one name and rendered decisions as to which was the proper, official designation.

Board decisions, in most cases, received general approval from the citizens and agencies concerned. This was not surprising because in its deliberations the board tried, with reasonable success, to select the name that enjoyed the most common usage and the widest public support. On the relatively few occasions that it ignored local usage and wishes in choosing between names—as it did in 1900 when it selected Porto Rico over Puerto Rico—the board's action set off fireworks of protest. In the case of Porto Rico the fireworks popped and crackled until 1932 when Congress, annoyed over the BGN's reluctance to correct what had been an obvious error in judgment, passed legislation restoring the name to Puerto Rico.

But if decisions between competing names were usually received calmly and approvingly, the principles the board laid down to govern the form of place-names were quite another matter. The purpose of the principles—to simplify and streamline names—seemed on the surface to be harmless enough, even commendable. It was the way in which this purpose was to be achieved that caused people to bristle like porcupines. Among other things, the principles specified that:

Apostrophes would be dropped from names wherever possible. Thus, Miller's Falls would become Millers Falls.

Names ending in "burgh" would drop the "h" so that the ending would become "burg."

Names including "borough" would abbreviate it to "boro."

Names consisting of more than one word would become compressed into a single word. Thus, Belle Haven would become Bellehaven.

The board should have known it was inviting trouble because—unlike decisions between competing names—the principles affected names that were not in dispute, names that were established and accepted in their present forms. Dr. Mendenhall and his colleagues should have realized that residents of a community would resent the long arm of government reaching into their midst to revise the hometown name they were contented with. The board might have looked back on history and heeded the experience of the Massachusetts General Court which, 250 years earlier, had stepped into a hornets' nest when it had tried to change the name of Marblehead.

The BGN decree making a single word out of multiple-word names met with only minor resentment in towns like Red Stone and Grand View that did not undergo radical change when transformed to Redstone and Grandview. But the effect was awkward and jarring when the BGN declared that places like Slippery Rock, Pennsylvania, and La Cynge, Kansas, were now Slipperyrock and Lacynge.

Stung by the widespread complaints it had precipitated, the board reconsidered and concluded that some multiple-word names simply did not lend themselves to compression into a single word—either because it created difficulty in readily determining the proper pronunciation or because it obscured the original meaning of the name. So the board wisely reversed itself on Slipperyrock, Lacynge, and similar names that were better left as separate words.

The two principles that seemed to be the least sweeping turned out to be the most troublesome for the board—dropping the *h* from burgh and dropping the apostrophe. That little *h* and even smaller apostrophe quickly became large thorns in the side of the BGN.

When the BGN published its principles in 1891 there were a half-dozen Pittsburghs in the nation that had borrowed their name from the original Pittsburgh in Pennsylvania. They fumed and they sputtered, but their hearts were not really in it because they had not conceived the name; they had merely borrowed it and thus neither their egos nor their pride of authorship was actually bruised by the edict. They put up only token resistance and then dropped their *h*. But in Pennsylvania the story was quite different. There was no halfhearted, token resistance in defense of the *h* in Pennsylvania's Pittsburgh where the *h* was serious business.

The Pennsylvanians had given birth to the name; it was their baby and they felt the deep attachment of parenthood. But there was also another powerful reason for them to cling pugnaciously to their *h*. Many of the original settlers had been Scottish and in conceiving the name they had accomplished two objectives related to the land of their birth. They had honored William Pitt, a British statesman admired by Scots, and they had honored Scotland itself by adding "burgh"—a typically Scottish ending— to Pitt. Just as long as Edinburgh, the capital of Scotland, retained its *h*—which would be as long as that city stood—the Pittsburghers would do battle to keep theirs. Furthermore, if "burgh" with an *h* was Scottish, "burg" without an *h* was Germanic, as in Hamburg, Augsburg, and Brandenburg. The Pittsburghers bore no particular animosity toward Germans but they were adamantly opposed to trading their rightful Scottish heritage for a counterfeit German one.

The battle lines were drawn. Pennsylvania mounted an editorial campaign in defense of the *h*. Federal maps and documents and the post office dropped the *h*, but local residents stubbornly retained it in their return addresses and in all their correspondence. Local delegations enlisted the aid of their congressmen in pressuring the Board on Geographic Names to concede that the *h* should not, would not, and could not be snipped out of Pittsburgh, Pennsylvania.

Both sides stuck to their guns. To reemphasize its position, the board in a February 16, 1900, message to President McKinley specifically noted that it had eliminated the Pennsylvanian *h*. But the Pennsylvanians, refusing to knuckle under, doggedly defended and used the *h*. Finally, in 1932, the Board on Geographic Names wearily raised the white flag of surrender. In its report that year to President Herbert Hoover the board reversed its long-held position and conceded that the proper, official spelling of the Pennsylvania city's name was indeed Pittsburgh.

At the same time that the BGN had been feuding with Pittsburgh over its *h* it had been engaged in an identical skirmish with the citizens of a city in New York. Founded by Scots in 1702, a half century before Pittsburgh, the settlers had styled their community Newburgh for the city of that name in their native Scotland. The Newburghers were as incensed as the Pittsburghers by the board's edict that the *h* be dropped from municipal titles that included "burgh." They fought the ban just as determinedly and eventually were as victorious as the Pittsburghers. The board caved in and restored the *h* to Newburgh.

If members of the BGN came to look on the *h* with marked unhappiness, the even smaller and seemingly less threatening apostrophe caused them at least as much grief. At first it seemed that the board's decree lopping off apostrophes would be accepted peacefully. The Post Office Department ruthlessly pruned it from names of its post offices; in 1894 alone the department snipped off 1,665 apostrophes. Compilers of commercial maps and atlases, publishers of railroad schedules, editors and educators followed the lead of the Post Office Department and dropped apostrophes left and right. The towns themselves, seeing everyone else strip them of their apostrophes, accepted the inevitable and followed suit whether they liked it or not. Except for one place—Martha's Vineyard, Massachusetts.

The Vineyarders doted on their apostrophe. It had been theirs ever since 1602 when Captain Bartholomew Gosnold discovered the Massachusetts island and named it Martha's Vineyard for its growth of wild grapevines and after his young daughter, Martha. Outraged by the BGN decision to strip them of the grammatical curlicue they had clung to for three centuries, the Vineyarders refused to submit. Flaunting their apostrophe like a battle flag, they counterattacked through the press and through their political representatives. Ultimately, like the Pittsburghers battling for their *h,* they were victorious. By odd coincidence, in its 1932 report to President Hoover—the same report in which it tossed in the towel on Pittsburgh's *h*—the board officially restored the apostrophe to Martha's Vineyard.

If the BGN thought that surrender in 1932 had finally put an end to its woes it was mistaken. The little apostrophe is still causing difficulties for the Board on Geographic Names. For many years Vermonters have campaigned to have the apostrophe returned to Thompson Point. As a matter of fact, the Vermonters have been fighting for both an apostrophe and an *s.* They want to get back both the apostrophe and the *s* that the board snipped away from the original Thompson's Point. After nibbling away at the BGN defenses unsuccessfully on a piecemeal basis for a number of years, residents in 1964 submitted to the board a firm, formal petition for restoration of their missing parts, basing their case on the use of *s* in their name for one hundred years and on the precedent established when the board returned the apostrophe to Martha's Vineyard.

The board considered the matter and issued a compromise

ruling that restored the *s* but not the apostrophe to the petitioners, thus making their name Thompsons Point. A half-victory
did not satisfy the Vermonters. They are still holding out for
Thompson's Point and are determined to get it, apostrophe and
all. On July 2, 1968, the state authorities of Vermont backed
up the Pointers by voting unanimous approval of Thompson's
Point as the authentic and proper name of the place. On the
basis of this official action, the Pointers submitted a new petition
to the board but it refused to reopen the case. Vermonters vow
the matter is not closed. They pledge to continue the fight until
the board gives them back their apostrophe.

Because it includes such appealing elements as humor and
as citizens taking on the bureaucracy, there is a temptation to
dwell on the BGN's difficulties and to skip past its accomplishments. To give in to this temptation would be to render an
injustice. When it came into being, the board assumed responsibility for a monumental task that had been continually growing
in size and complexity ever since the first white man came to
these shores. Under the circumstances the surprise is not that
the board occasionally tripped over its own feet as it tried to
hack a way through the thicket, but that it was able to clear a
pathway.

In 1900 Henry Gannett, then chairman of the board, reported to President McKinley that probably less than half of all
U.S. place-names had remained unchanged and undisputed
since they were first conceived. Then he proceeded to recount
the causes of this confusion and conflict. He pointed to the
astonishingly large number of instances in which, through
either ignorance or carelessness, place-names had been entered
inaccurately in official records. He enumerated the multitude
of cases in which succeeding waves of settlers had created new
geographic names for places that had already been named by
their predecessors. He lamented the frequency with which railroads and post offices had selected place-names different from
each other's and different from the one employed by local resi-

dents. Turning to Indian names that had been preserved, Gannett said—sadly, one suspects—that they had "everywhere been a fruitful source of differences in spelling, inasmuch as no two persons alike render into the same English characters the obscure sounds of Indian names."

Although he did not do so, Gannett could have included another factor that complicated the work of the board—its lack of personnel and of budget. The man who preceded him in office, Mendenhall, was not so reticent on this point. He wrote the President in 1891 that the board

> has no means of providing for printing and circulating its decisions. . . . Through the courtesy of the Smithsonian Institution, and at its expense, Bulletin No. 1 has been published, and an edition of 7,000 copies distributed. The Coast and Geodetic Survey has printed its second bulletin with an edition of 7,500 copies, and the Lighthouse Board has through the Treasury Department printed the third bulletin, with an edition of 8,000 copies. This method of publication is obviously unsatisfactory . . . and the Board asks that recommendation be made to the Congress that proper provision be made for printing and distributing these bulletins.

Only once since it was created in 1890 has the Board on Geographic Names been allotted both a staff and funds on a generous scale and that was under the stress of wartime emergency. At the outbreak of World War II, with every corner of the globe an actual or potential battlefield, there was an urgent need for worldwide maps with uniform, standardized place-names to forestall confusion within the military forces and between the Allies.

Achieving standardization was enormously complicated by the fact that thousands upon thousands of foreign place-names had never been rendered in the Roman alphabet and existed only in such non-Roman writing systems as those of the Chinese, the Japanese, the Koreans, the Arabs, and the Russians. The board plunged into the awesome task, devising methods of rendering foreign writing systems into the Roman alphabet and compiling standardized place-names for the vast military map requirements. Despite the intense pressure of this wartime responsibility the board did not interrupt, or even diminish, its domestic name endeavors.

There is no chance that the United States Board on Geographic Names will ever complete its task and thus work itself out of existence even though it currently considers some 600 geographic name problems each month. So far it has published its approved form of more than 3,000,000 U.S. place-names, but there is always fresh grist for its mill because new towns are established, or established towns seek to adopt new names, or fresh evidence reveals that an existing place-name is inaccurate or inappropriate. And then, of course, there are always those Vermonters trying to get the apostrophe put back into Thompsons Point.

7

Name-Droppers

Americans have demonstrated—as the Board on Geographic Names discovered, and as the Massachusetts General Court had discovered back in 1630 when it tried to eliminate Marblehead —that they will usually close ranks to resist stubbornly efforts to tamper with their hometown names.

But there is another side to that coin. Paradoxically, Americans have also demonstrated that loyalty to place-name can be fickle and fleeting. If they have been reluctant to discard an established place-name, they have also very frequently been quick to make a change. This contradiction in attitudes seems to hinge on the question of who gets the idea to make the change. If the proposal for municipal name-dropping originates locally that is one thing. But if the pressure to impose change originates among outsiders it generates resistance.

It is usually a simple enough matter to recognize what it is that prompts people to erase their place-name and write in a fresh one as a substitute. Consider, for example, the situation that confronted a community in Minnesota. The town had its origin in 1840 as a crude cabin built by Pierre Parrant, a hard-bitten French-Canadian whose one ambition in life appeared to be to sell as much whiskey as possible to the fur traders and soldiers passing through the region. A tough, slippery individual no better than the rotgut whiskey he dispensed, he was called Pig's Eye by his customers who gave him their business only because their thirst was great and there was no other source of supply in the vicinity. Gradually a small settlement grew up around the cabin, and it came to be called Pig's Eye for its most notorious resident.

The first breath of respectability—one could say the first sober breath—wafted over the community of Pig's Eye when a priest came to town and built a small log church to serve the region. Soon afterward a few churchgoing families arrived to take up permanent residence there. Pig's Eye became less and less suitable to designate a place that was starting to grow into a stable, responsible town so the residents voted to eliminate it and instead to style the community after its church—St. Paul.

What happened to Pig's Eye/St. Paul, Minnesota, happened to many another place as its rough edges began to be worn away and civilizing influences came into play. The citizens simply discovered that their place-names—chosen with no thought of tomorrow—were too outlandish, too jarring when tomorrow did come.

It happened in Montana where Pair o' Dice became Paradise. It happened in New Mexico where Riley's Switch became Clovis, and in Maryland where Johnnycake became Catonsville. In California, Hangtown became Placerville, and Bedbug emerged —sanitized and scrubbed—as Ione. Hell-to-Pay, Washington, transformed itself into Eltopia; Frog Level, South Carolina, achieved a new look by becoming Prosperity; and Shoe Heel, North Carolina, became Maxton. A small hamlet in West Virginia elevated itself all the way from Mole Hill to Mountain, while over in Kentucky a community traded in its sweaty image as Hot Spot for the much more comfortable atmosphere of Premium.

The attempt to name-drop its way into municipal respectability was not always smooth sailing for every town that tried it. Occasionally, there was a booby trap lurking along the route toward place-name dignity, as a group of Pennsylvanians learned when they laid out their town in 1812. They designated their settlement Meansville for William Mean, the most prominent of the founders. Very soon, they discovered to their discomfort that their choice had made them the butt of jokes. Neighbors all around them never missed an opportunity to refer to the residents of Meansville as the "mean people." The passage of time did nothing to diminish the gibes; on the contrary, as time elapsed the jokes became a permanent fixture.

Finally, their patience exhausted, the citizens decided to put an end to the wisecracks about their "meanness." They dropped Meansville and for it substituted Towanda, a name that long departed Indians had once employed locally. The jokes ended. But only for a little while. A language scholar who came along translated Towanda as "Place where we bury the dead." Then the unlucky residents had to learn to live with a fresh round of jokes about being the graveyard for mean people.

In name-dropping, as in everything else, there were always some rugged individualists like Ezra Meeker who enjoyed swimming against the tide. Meeker had no sympathy for the widespread desire to attain place-name dignity; what he doted on was the unconventional, vigorous name, the one with the verve and the sparkle of originality.

His home town—Franklin, Washington—had the kind of unimaginative, bland title that rubbed him the wrong way, so in 1877 Meeker decided to do something about it. He selected a distinctive substitute, one that would not be shared with any other town in existence—Puyallup, from the Indian meaning "generous people." It wasn't the meaning that was so attractive to Meeker but rather the unusual sequence of letters that would make it plain to everyone that here was no name to be taken lightly and to be spoken with glib fluency. Because Meeker was the most influential man in town he encountered no obstacles in adopting Puyallup as a replacement for Franklin.

Like Ezra Meeker, the residents of the Virginia hamlet of Tightsqueeze enjoyed swimming against the tide; they were delighted with their unconventional place-name. They insisted good-humoredly that their off-beat name was coined before the Civil War to mark the exploits of a sharp dealing shopkeeper who sold local farmers whiskey in one-gallon jugs but charged them for two gallons by maintaining that he had made a "right tight squeeze" to get it all in. After more than a century of contented existence as Tightsqueeze, the little town awoke one morning to learn that the county authorities—seeking greater place-name dignity within their borders—had arbitrarily switched Tightsqueeze to Fairview. The Tightsqueezers bellowed their outrage so lustily that the county authorities hastily restored their cherished name to them.

Occasionally, name-dropping came about impulsively in an unplanned, spontaneous gesture that did not result from dissatisfaction with an existing name. For almost two centuries a small town in North Carolina was quite content to be called Brinkley. No voice had ever been raised, even faintly, to criticize the place-name. Then, as Brinkley entered the twentieth century, the most exciting event ever to transpire in the quiet little community occurred—electricity came to town. Jolted out of their drowsiness by the marvels of electricity, the residents decided that they had to devise a permanent reminder of this high point in local history. In a spur-of-the-moment action, they agreed to drop Brinkley and replace it with Delco, the name of the company that had manufactured their wonderful electric generator.

The same impulse to use their place-name as a local historic marker swept over a group of Oklahomans. They had no fault to find with their long-established name—Berwyn. They liked its solid sound, the way it lay comfortably on their tongues. But one of their citizens had created a local sensation by moving to Hollywood where he became a cowboy movie star and they felt an obligation to memorialize their most famous local son; it occurred to them, as it had to the Brinkleyites, that a place-name can become a convenient, economical historic marker. So Berwyn, Oklahoma, became Gene Autry.

Municipal name-dropping did not always come in one single break with the past; sometimes it developed by stages. The first permanent settlers at a site in Pennsylvania, choosing a place-name that reflected the difficulty of eking out a living there, called it Skunk's Misery. In 1800 the picture began to look a little brighter when Ebenezer and Benjamin Slocum came to Skunk's Misery to establish a forge and a distillery. Because Skunk's Misery did not seem to be a name that would help the new businesses prosper, the residents dropped it in favor of the more substantial Unionville. Later, in a gesture of gratitude to the men upon whom they depended for their jobs, they switched to Slocum's Hollow. Unfortunately, it turned out to be a mean-ingless gesture because in a few years the Slocum enterprises failed and the Slocums left for greener pastures.

Then, in 1840, two other brothers—Selden and George Scranton—arrived and built a new, improved forge that began to flourish almost at once. The resurrected community, having seen the last of the Slocums, renamed itself Harrison for President William H. Harrison. Soon, however, the Scranton forge —like the Slocum forge before it—was in trouble. But this trouble was different. The Scrantons were victims of success— their forge had booked so many orders that it had to be ex-panded rapidly to fill them, and the Scrantons had insufficient capital to finance expansion. A wealthy cousin, Joseph H. Scranton, provided the funds and assumed the presidency of the company. The new head of the company decided that since he was the one who had come to the rescue there was no reason for Harrison to reap the place-name glory so he renamed the town Scrantonia for himself. Later he dropped the fancy ending and made it plain Scranton.

The multiple changes that began with Skunk's Misery and finally ended with Scranton must take a backseat to another Pennsylvania town that surely is a prime candidate for the name-dropping championship. It was established in 1811 as Scrabble-town. Soon the residents had second thoughts about their place-name; they dropped Scrabbletown and replaced it with Coalville. Then, tiring of Coalville, they switched to Skunk-town. Nobody can blame them for dropping Skunktown, but it is a bit difficult to see any greater merit in the new name they chose—Peestone. There were no expressions of regret when the residents made another change, this time to Hightown. Still fickle, they continued to make more changes. From Hightown they became Hendricksburg, then Nanticoke Junction, and then Alberts. Finally, sixty years after they had started out as Scrabbletown, the citizens grew bored with their long ride on the place-name merry-go-round so they adopted their tenth and final title, styling themselves Ashley for a prominent local family.

While the urge to achieve linguistic respectability inspired much of the American fondness for municipal name-dropping, sometimes the changes stemmed from motives that were less praiseworthy. Take the case of Hot Springs, New Mexico, as an example. During the waning days of the golden age of radio, before the microphone was dethroned by the television camera, one of the most popular programs broadcast nationally was the zany *Truth or Consequences*. A group of Hot Springs business-men, anxious to increase the flow of tourists to their town, con-ceived a way to cash in on the program's popularity. By adopting the show's title as their place-name, they reasoned, they were bound to reap enormous publicity that would put them on the tourist map. The show's promoters fell in readily with the idea, agreeing to plug the town during their broadcasts, because they knew that they too would benefit from the publicity. So venerable Hot Springs was dropped and *Truth or Consequences* was adopted as its offbeat replacement in pursuit of tourist dollars.

What transpired in Shawneetown, Arkansas, was considerably more slippery than the *Truth or Consequences* escapade. Named for the Shawnee Indians who had once occupied the site, Shawneetown was a historically appropriate designation and the residents were quite satisfied with it. Then along came the congressional election campaign of 1850. The hotly contested struggle for the congressional seat representing the Shawneetown district pitted two evenly matched candidates against each other. Casting about for a way to gain an advantage over his opponent, one of the rivals—Archibald Yell—hatched a scheme to have Shawneetown renamed for him on the theory that the resulting publicity would help him at the ballot box. He quietly slipped fifty dollars to a few local go-betweens as a bribe to drum up enthusiasm for the switch. They drummed so effectively that Shawneetown became Yellsville. It would be nice to say that tainted tactics never succeed and that Yell was defeated at the polls. The truth is that Yell gained a majority in Yellsville and went on to Congress.

Like Archibald Yell, the town fathers of Twin Forks, Washington, had a tainted motive in engineering a change in their municipal name. The problem in Twin Forks was not political but economic. The local economy was sagging badly and the town was seeking a means of restoring a measure of financial health to Twin Forks. One after the other, proposals were considered and discarded. Then someone suggested that funds for the town might be wrung out of its name. Surely, the idea went, if Twin Forks were renamed for a wealthy man, a *very* wealthy man, and if the mayor wrote a letter notifying him of the honor and at the same time delicately describing the economic plight of the town, then he would undoubtedly feel obligated to make a generous donation to his municipal namesake. The city fathers studied a list of American millionaires and picked out George D. Pullman, inventor of the railroad sleeping car, as the pigeon to be plucked. Twin Forks promptly rechristened itself Pullman and a suitable letter was sent off. Eventually, a polite reply was received. With it came a check for fifty dollars. What the crestfallen schemers had failed to realize was that the cards were stacked against them from the beginning. George Pullman already had a city named for him—Pullman, Illinois.

A North Dakota town—Edwinton—suffered from the same kind of economic pinch as Twin Forks/Pullman and the residents came up with the same kind of scheme to use the place-name as a money machine. But the North Dakotans were more ambitious than the citizens of Twin Forks—they set their sights not on a single American millionaire but on a whole nation. One of the wealthiest countries in the world at the time was Germany and the Edwintonians dearly wanted to see some of the German riches invested in their local economy. A thoroughly Germanic place-name, they figured, ought to make their town an attractive candidate for German investment capital. So, coveting German wealth, the North Dakotans dumped Edwinton and styled their town Bismarck after Prince Otto von Bismarck, chancellor of Germany. The Germans were flattered, but not sufficiently so to make investments in the renamed town. Having rung up "No Sale" on its municipal cash register and stuck with a name it really hadn't wanted, Bismarck muddled through and in time flourished as the capital of North Dakota.

Unlike the North Dakotans who name-dropped their way into a Germanic place-name, a group of Michiganders name-dropped their way out of one. From the time it was founded in 1830 until the outbreak of World War I, the citizens of Berlin, Michigan, had no fault to find with their municipal title. But after the Kaiser's troops marched on France their Germanic name became an acute embarrassment to them because they were wholeheartedly rooting for France to whip the Germans. To make their sentiments unmistakably clear they dropped Berlin and renamed their town Marne for the place in France where Marshal Joffre halted the German advance on Paris in 1914.

The evidence is quite plain that for the last couple of centuries Americans have been exhibiting ingenuity in name-dropping their way toward a wide variey of goals ranging from attaining municipal dignity or linguistic uniqueness to stuffing ballot boxes or cash registers to delivering an international slap in the face. Sometimes their place-name gamesmanship was played out with complete success, sometimes with only marginal success or even failure, but seldom was it played out with dullness.

8

The Phantoms

Cousins to the place-names that were dropped are names that remained while their places were dropped. Some names linger like tattered banners over deserted parade grounds. Once those places had been vigorous, lusty mining settlements, or rest stops for wagon trains, stagecoaches, cattle drives, or marketing centers for farmers, or fledgling communities clustered around mill or forge. Then mines and wagon trains petered out, railroads displaced stage coaches, rival markets claimed the farmer, the mill stopped turning and the forge grew cold. Sometimes it was simply a matter of the people moving on.

Whatever the reason, voices fell silent and life ebbed from the settlements. . . . Only weed-choked cemeteries, gaping basement holes, derelict buildings remained to mark what once had been. And the place-names remained too—on the maps and in the records—to mark what had been but was no longer.

Though some had become phantom place-names, not all subsided into insignificance. It's hard to be indifferent about such ghostly names as Cuddy Hunk, Mississippi; Silver Reef, Utah; Marrowbone, Kentucky; Cracker's Neck, Georgia; and Jangling Plains, Connecticut. What about ghosts like Gouge Eye and Brandy Gulch, or another California phantom, Jackass Hill, which was a community of three-thousand during Gold Rush days? Now Jackass Hill is only a place-name and what is left of the cabin where Mark Twain wintered in 1864.

Settlers who changed their minds and pulled up stakes to strike out again, abandoning their place-names behind them, swelled the legion of phantoms. Even more numerous were the Indian phantoms. Indian tribes were largely nomadic, so many of their place-names were fated to become ghosts when the tribe moved on. Occasionally when whites came across a phantom Indian name that struck their fancy they adopted it and gave it a new life. White settlers who founded a town in Pennsylvania breathed fresh vitality into the phantom place-name left behind by departed Indian villagers—Moosic, "place of the elk." Far to the northwest in what is now the state of Washington other settlers resurrected for their community the red ghost of Walla Walla, "place of many waters."

But if some came on the American scene early to revive old ghosts, others were on the scene almost as early to create new ones. London Town, Maryland, was laid out in the mid-1600s and quickly attracted attention as a promising trading center for farmers and shipping point for tobacco. London Town thrived for a century until it was overwhelmed by competition from nearby Annapolis. The town passed its peak and began to decline. It managed to hold on until after the Revolution, then, soon after the nation was born, London Town quietly expired. All that remains today is a pre-Revolutionary brick mansion built by a wealthy merchant, a log tobacco barn, and the place-name.

In Georgia it was the railroad that drained the life from Troupville, named for Governor George M. Troup. When the railroad came to the area in 1859 its tracks capriciously bypassed the town by a dozen miles. Because the railroad was the passport to progress and growth, the residents deserted Troupville. Moving everything that could be dismantled, they reassembled the town beside the track. Leaving their place-name behind to preside over the deserted site, they turned to their old source of inspiration— Governor Troup—for their new name, styling themselves Valdosta for the governor's plantation, Val d'Aosta.

For a special kind of ghostliness one must turn to the place-names of the western desert that mark places which did not exist, never had, and never would. These phantoms were created by men enticed from the East Coast and Europe by the lure of California gold. The desolate, fiercely hot wasteland took a heavy toll of those gold-struck Forty-niners. Hundreds perished from thirst, heat, sickness, or crushing fatigue. The survivors buried the dead where they fell, and, so they would not lie in an unknown place in an empty wasteland, named the spot and then moved on. When they reached the West Coast they wrote the families of their dead companions to tell them the body had been buried in the western desert in a place named Endurance or Fortitude or Last Gasp—place-names that were only figments of their imagination and tombs for the dead.

At the opposite extreme from those phantom place-names that existed only as a state of mind are those that existed for a time as an actual state, however lacking their official recognition. The first of these rump states came into being in the mountainous, western region of North Carolina.

The inhabitants of the three Carolina counties in the west were North Carolinians in name but not in spirit. Their loyalty to the state had been drained away by a long period of neglect at the hands of the North Carolina authorities. Their anger mounted as state officials resolutely stayed on the other side of the mountains and left them to fend for themselves. In 1784, tired of their frustrating role as stepchildren of the state, the residents convened in Jonesboro to take matters into their own hands. In this assembly, and in others that followed shortly, they declared themselves to be citizens of the new State of Franklin and they proceeded to establish all the organs of state government. They elected John Sevier their governor for a three-year period, adopted a constitution, established courts, appointed magistrates, levied taxes, and adopted state laws.

Stung into action, North Carolina officials finally crossed the mountains they had shunned for so long and tried to reestablish their authority. The Franklinites ignored the North Carolinians. In 1790 Congress stepped in to settle the dispute, first designating Franklin a territory, and then, in 1796, linking the territory to an adjoining region and admitting the whole to the Union as the State of Tennessee.

The State of Franklin had joined the ranks of the phantom place-names, but as a constant reminder of its lively history a county in the newly created State of Tennessee styled itself Franklin.

In 1848 Mormons who had settled a remote region some 1,500 miles west of Franklin petitioned Congress to organize them into a territory as a preliminary to granting statehood. When Congress failed to act on the request, the petitioners borrowed a page from Franklin's book by declaring themselves to be the Provisional State of Deseret, a Mormon word meaning "honeybee." Getting right down to the business of self-declared statehood, the Desereters promptly appointed a full slate of state officials to conduct the affairs of their government. Scorning this attempt to force its hand, Congress withheld recognition from Deseret and its officials. Instead, in 1850 Congress molded the region into the Territory of Utah, adopting the name for a local Indian tribe, the Uttahih. Deseret's organs of government, ignored by Washington and superseded by properly constituted agencies, disappeared. To emphasize its displeasure, Congress waited forty-six more years before it transformed Utah from a territory to a state.

A short time after Deseret had become a ghostly place-name, a delegation representing inhabitants of an adjoining area called on Congress for creation of territorial status for themselves as a prelude to statehood. When Congress failed to respond promptly, the impatient inhabitants designated themselves the Territory of Jefferson and elected their own territorial governor and officials. Congress had by this time made it quite clear that it would permit nobody to short-cut its exclusive power to create territories and states. In 1861, two years after Jefferson had constituted itself, Congress released the wind from the Jefferson balloon—as it had deflated Franklin and Deseret earlier—by ignoring its rump government and organizing the Jeffersonians into Colorado Territory.

Franklin, Deseret, and Jefferson occupy positions of prominence in the parade of place-name phantoms. Other ghostly names simply mark sites where settlements were born, lived for a while, and then died, but Franklin, Deseret and Jefferson were not concerned with mere settlements. They mark places where the dreams were larger, the aspirations more pretentious. Even so, for all their pretensions none had greater visions of grandeur than a Yankee movement that has been almost forgotten.

A large, sprawling township in the northernmost sector of New Hampshire, Pittsburg had for a long time been in the unenviable position of being claimed by two masters. Because the border between New Hampshire and British Canada was ill-defined and vague, both jurisdictions laid claim to Pittsburg and the hapless township was caught in the middle. The Revolutionary War established the sovereignty and independence of the United States, but it failed to pin down ownership of the disputed Pittsburg region.

Finally, in 1832, the Pittsburgers decided the only way to end their unhappy situation as an international yo-yo was to cut the string themselves. So the Pittsburgers notified the United States that their township was not a part of the United States, and they notified Canada it was not a part of Canada. In fact, they declared, Pittsburg was no longer simply a township. It had become, the Pittsburgers said, an independent nation—the Indian Stream Republic. Then the world's newest would-be nation proceeded to adopt a constitution, to elect an executive council and a legislature, to promulgate a legal code, and to create a judicial system.

For three years the Indian Stream Republic carried on as though it were sovereign, maintaining—to the extent that its meager resources permitted—many of the trappings of nationhood. Meanwhile, the border dispute between the United States and Canada continued unabated and even escalated to the point where there was talk of war to settle the matter. At stake was not only the area that had declared itself to be an independent republic; at stake was disputed territory stretching all the way from the Atlantic to Minnesota.

In 1835, units of the New Hampshire militia marched into the Indian Stream Republic, encountering no armed opposition because there was no Indian Stream army to offer opposition. Bowing to the inevitable, the Indian Stream Republic quietly departed from the family of nations and became once again the township of Pittsburg. Elsewhere, American and British statesmen sat down together to sort out the territorial problem and to fashion a solution to it. The negotiations were protracted but finally, in 1842, the Webster-Ashburton Treaty was signed fixing the American-Canadian border along a mutually acceptable line. Among other provisions of the treaty, it confirmed Pittsburg township as a part of New Hampshire. The parade of the phantom place-names had gained a pretentious new member—the Indian Stream Republic. There is no denying that it added a touch of class, in a comic opera sort of way, to the line-up.

The Indian Stream Republic was neither the first nor the only area that established itself for a time as a republic before submitting to the sovereignty of the United States. Three other places that did function for a period as republics—California, Texas, and Vermont—never relinquished their names to the legion of phantoms because their place-names never became empty shells.

But another that aspired to nationhood did become an empty shell. If the Indian Stream Republic's foray into nationhood had contained elements of comedy, this one was sheer, unrelieved tragedy. It required four long, hard years of bitter warfare and a total of perhaps one million dead and wounded on both sides before the Confederate States of America assumed its place at the head of the procession of place-name phantoms.

9

Ink, Ark., and All That

There are whole libraries of scholarly works and statistical surveys that tell America's story, but a few can recount the tale in quite the way that the people unconsciously do themselves in revealing their own story through their own place-names.

It is in those place-names and in what lies behind them that one catches glimpses—fleeting, perhaps, but very real—of the nature, the gusto, the quirks, the adventures and misadventures, the essence of the nation and those who built it. Others have written the biography of the nation, but America has fashioned her own autobiography in her place-names. Here are a few excerpts from that engaging story.

ACCIDENT, MARYLAND. In 1751 George II of England, short of cash, wiped out a debt to George Deakins by granting him six hundred acres of land in western Maryland. Under terms of the grant Deakins could claim whichever six hundred acres he wished. A shrewd individual, Deakins hired two separate sets of engineers to survey the area for the choicest acreage, keeping each team in ignorance of the fact that he had hired another for the same purpose. After Deakins received both reports he compared them and was astonished to find that each team had selected the identical tract. Considering it to be an accident arranged by a fate that was watching out for his best interests, Deakins named it "The Accidental Tract" and the town that eventually developed there adopted its name from that.

ANNISTON, ALABAMA. Most cities grow slowly, but Anniston was created almost overnight. In 1872 a group of northern and southern investors, not letting the recently concluded Civil War get in the way of profit, joined forces to organize the Woodstock Iron Company to exploit iron deposits at the site. Bringing in hundreds of architects, engineers and craftsmen, and tons of machinery and materials, they built the city from scratch—streets, water and sewage systems, houses, schools, churches, shops, even a hotel. Simultaneously, of course, they built the industrial plant to smelt and process the ore. In all the turmoil and hustle it took a half-dozen years before the board of directors realized they had forgotten to name the city. Because the town was a creation of the Woodstock Iron Company—lock, stock, and smelter—the directors concluded it was only fitting to call it Woodstock, and in 1879 they applied for a local post office to be established in that name. Postal authorities rejected the application because a small community in Alabama had already styled itself in that way. Prevented from naming their city for the company that owned it, the directors did the next best thing: they named it for the wife of the company president—Annie Scott Tyler—dubbing it Anniston, a more polished version of Annie's Town.

APPLETON, MINNESOTA. Early French traders searching for furs penetrated a region new to them. Taking careful note of everything they saw, they found that the local Indians dug a potatolike root as a major part of their diet. The traders mapped the site and, with straightforward directness, labeled it Pomme de Terre, "potato." Years later, pioneer families who settled there accepted the place-name for their community, but they could not quite resist the urge to place their own imprint on it, so they decided to translate it from French into English. Unfortunately, their language ability was not quite equal to their intention. They mistranslated Pomme de Terre as "apple." Attaching a stem to the apple, they added "ton" at the end, winding up with Appleton.

AUBURN, WASHINGTON. The first permanent settlers, arriving in 1887, named their community Slaughter in honor of Lieutenant W. A. Slaughter who had gained some fame in the region as a courageous officer during the Indian wars. The town prospered and within a few years had grown large enough to justify building its first hotel. Until that time the residents had reacted good-naturedly to the wisecracks of visitors who thought Slaughter an amusing name for a town. But with the opening of the new hotel—The Slaughter House—the jokes multiplied as travelers laughed without restraint at the town that sent its visitors to The Slaughter House. No longer able to shrug off the gibes, the residents became thoroughly fed up with their unhappy role as the target for jokesters. The state legislature came to the rescue in 1893, passing an act that dropped Slaughter in favor of the more jokeproof Auburn. The first sign hauled down was the one over the hotel.

AUSTERLITZ, NEW YORK. In 1824 a town in upstate New York became incorporated as Waterloo, naming itself for the spectacular battle of nine years earlier in which Wellington had dealt Napoleon a crushing defeat. Many Americans, mindful of the aid France had rendered during the Revolution, were angry that any place in the nation would style itself in a way that emphasized a bleak period in French history. Few were quite as angry as the resident of another New York town, Martin Van

Buren, who would, in 1837, become President of the United States. Van Buren, an enthusiastic admirer of France, never softened his anger toward his fellow New Yorkers in Waterloo. His moment of sweet revenge came when his own community, previously unnamed, became large enough to assume its own municipal title. At his instigation, and to the unrestrained glee of all who felt as he did, the town christened itself Austerlitz for the place in Czechoslovakia where, in 1805, Napoleon had won a smashing victory over the combined Russian and Austrian armies.

AVONDALE, RHODE ISLAND. Catastrophe struck a Rhode Island shipowner when his vessel sank in a violent storm in 1749, carrying all of his cash resources to a watery grave. The only thing of material value remaining to him was a tract of land. In order to make a fresh start he had to convert the land into cash as quickly and as profitably as possible. Conceiving a plan that would suit his purpose, he petitioned the general assembly for permission to divide his tract into building lots and to raffle them off in a lottery. Permission was granted, the land was cut into 124 parcels, and enough lottery tickets were sold to restore the shipowner to financial health. The winners built homes on their parcels of land and—with simple honesty—called their village Lotteryville. For a century and a half Lotteryville mellowed and slowly grew, and in 1893 the residents asked that a local post office be established. The postal authorities were agreeable, but only on condition that Lotteryville abandon its name since federal law prohibits lotteries. In order to get their post office, the Lotteryvillians reluctantly dropped the name that commemorated a legal lottery held at a time before there was a federal government and federal laws, adopted bland Avondale in its place, and satisfied the demands of bureaucracy.

BANGOR, MAINE. The city owes its name to the Reverend Seth Noble who was known widely for two of his most cherished hobbies: drinking whiskey and singing hymns whenever he was in his cups, which was fairly often. His neighbors winked at his weaknesses because many shared them, at least his drinking if not his hymn-singing, and because the Reverend Mr. Noble was a likable sort—cheerful, friendly, always ready to lend a hand even though that hand might be a trifle unsteady. In 1791, their population having grown to 500, the residents decided to petition the state legislature for incorporation as the town of Sunbury and they selected the Reverend Mr. Noble to present their request. When the preacher appeared before the clerk of the legislature he was in a pleasant alcoholic glow happily singing his favorite hymn. Asked by the clerk what name had been chosen for the town, Noble impulsively blurted out the name of the hymn that was on his lips: Bangor. Surprised by the switch, but tolerant of and amused by their preacher, the residents displayed no anger over Bangor.

BARRE, VERMONT. Each of the founders of the town insisted that he be granted the privilege of selecting its name. The argument persisted for a time and then gradually, their resolve worn away by the long dispute, the contenders dropped out until there were only two left. Neither would give an inch, each determined to name the town for the place from which he had come to Vermont to live. Their tempers grew frayed and the argument more heated. A fistfight broke out between the pair. They slugged it out until one lay unconscious. The winner was a man from Barre, Massachusetts. The town was awarded the Massachusetts name by a knockout.

BATON ROUGE, LOUISIANA. The French-Canadian naval officer and colonizer, Pierre le Moyne, sieur d'Iberville, exploring the lower Mississippi River valley in 1699, was the first European to reach there. In his journals he noted that the site was the boundary point between two Indian tribes and that the tribes marked it by a large, red stick they had driven into the ground.

Iberville indicated the spot on his map, labeling it Baton Rouge, "red stick." Twenty years later a French force built a fort at the site and assumed the place-name that Iberville had bestowed on it; the town that eventually emerged retained it.

BICKNELL, UTAH. The village was getting along contentedly as Thurber until 1917 when a wealthy, eccentric New Yorker— Thomas W. Bicknell—offered to donate a library to any place in Utah that would in return rename itself Bicknell in his honor. Thurber, willing enough to swap names in order to get a free library, jumped at the offer. The rub was that Grayson, Utah, jumped at the same time. One library but two towns that wanted to become Bicknell in order to claim it. What to do? The compromise worked out was worthy of Solomon: Thurber became Bicknell, Grayson became Blanding after Mrs. Bicknell's maiden name, and the books were divided equally between both towns. (This wasn't the first time that a library was used to snag a place-name. In 1803, when a Maine community was preparing to become an incorporated town a Boston doctor—Elijah Dix— promised to provide a municipal library to the town if it would immortalize him by incorporating as Dixfield. The local authorities agreed, officially naming the community Dixfield. But there were outraged cries when the "library" arrived from Boston. It consisted only of a single crate containing Dr. Dix's old medical books, left over from his days as a student.)

BLANDFORD, MASSACHUSETTS. When William Shirley—a man of whimsical impulses—was named to the governorship of Massachusetts in 1741, one of his official acts was to issue a spur-of-the-moment order that the town of Glasgow be renamed Blandford for the ship that had brought him from England. The residents of Glasgow—mainly Scots who had honored the land of their birth by styling themselves after its largest city—were furious over the decision to swap their proud Scottish name for that of an insignificant English sailing vessel. They staged a protest meeting that framed a petition to Governor Shirley to cancel his order and they issued a plea to Scotland to rally to their defense. Back from Scotland came expressions of strong support for the cause of the Scottish-Americans and a pledge to donate a bell to their town hall if the American Glasgow were allowed to retain its name. Governor Shirley, unmoved by the pleas, insisted that his whimsical order be carried out.

BOWLING GREEN, KENTUCKY. Two brothers, Robert and George Moore, built adjoining homes there shortly after the Revolution. Others followed, and in a few years enough had settled at the site to warrant the county court holding sessions there at regularly scheduled intervals. The court sessions were held in Robert Moore's house. To relax during recesses, court officials and visiting lawyers amused themselves by playing bowls on the lawn behind Moore's house. There was little else to do for amusement in the small community, so the custom caught on with the residents and the bowling green became the focal point for their social life. When the time came to pick a place-name, Bowling Green seemed a natural choice.

CAMBRIDGE, MASSACHUSETTS. Lamenting the colony's limited educational facilities, the magistrates of the General Court of Massachusetts decided in 1636 to establish its first college, appropriating a modest sum for that purpose. At almost the same moment a Boston minister died. When his will was read it was found that he had bequeathed his extensive library and half of his considerable fortune to the college the court was then in the process of creating. Because the money he contributed was four times greater than their official appropriation, the grateful magistrates ordered that the college be called Harvard for the minister, the Reverend John Harvard. The court directed that Harvard College be built across the Charles River opposite Boston in New Towne, a fortified strong-point. As a further gesture of gratitude toward the Reverend Mr. Harvard, the court also ordered that

92

New Towne be renamed Cambridge for the English university town where the minister had been educated.

CANDO, NORTH DAKOTA. It was only a small, unnamed village in 1884 when the county commissioners met there to consider designating it as the county seat. Other communities within the county clamored for that honor, so the question had become a lively political issue. The meeting room was crowded and it was obvious to the commissioners from the very outset that they were in for a rough session. As the meeting progressed, the commissioners were constantly heckled by residents of other communities shouting the praises of their hometowns. Several times the audience interrupted the proceedings to argue that the matter of selecting a county seat could be settled only by a public vote and not by a decision of the commissioners. Annoyed by the frequent interruptions and by the attempts to dictate to them what they could and could not do, the commissioners became increasingly angry. Finally, the chairman boiled over, blurting out, "We'll show you what we can do. Not only will we make this the county seat, but we'll also name it Cando to show you what we can do." The decision of the commissioners stuck.

CANTON, MASSACHUSETTS. When the early settlers cast about for a suitable place-name, one of their number who was more influential—and more peculiar—than the rest insisted that it must be named for Canton, China. It was not that he held any special regard for the Chinese city. It was simply that he had calculated that if you started digging a hole in the town square and continued digging straight through the center of the earth you would emerge in Canton, China. It seemed to him that it would be a neat bit of symmetry to have a Canton at each end of the hole.

CINCINNATI, OHIO. In 1778 a group of pioneers liked the looks of a grassy bank opposite the mouth of the Licking River and agreed that this was the place where they would sink their roots. Pitching camp, they got right to work laying out streets, building cabins, and christening the settlement Columbia for the discoverer of America. But almost at once, one of the founders—Dr. John Filson, a man with a scholarly turn of mind—persuaded his companions to switch to a name he felt had more academic elegance than Columbia. The name Dr. Filson invented was a curious patchwork of English, Greek, Latin and French. Starting with the L from Licking River, he added os, Greek for "mouth"; anti, Latin for "opposite!"; and ville, French for "city." What he ended up with was the ponderous, multilingual Losantiville, "city opposite the mouth of the Licking River." Two years later, General Arthur St. Clair, governor of the Northwest Territory and devoted member of the Society of the Cincinnati, a patriotic society of officers who had served during the Revolution, arrived for an official inspection. Legend has it that the first words General St. Clair uttered when he entered town were, "Damn it, Losantiville is a terrible name. Change it to Cincinnati." Whether or not those were his actual words, his edict was obeyed.

CIRCLEVILLE, OHIO. When they laid it out in 1810 the founders were determined to give their town an air of distinction by making it different from any other place they had ever seen. To accomplish this, they started by making the town "square" a circle. Then they laid out two completely circular streets girdling the "square" and using it as a hub. Radiating outward from the hub like the spokes of a wheel were four cross-streets leading to the two outer circles. Naturally, the town was called Circleville. In 1846, finally tired of going around in circles, the townspeople straightened out their curves but retained their no longer descriptive place-name.

CLOVIS, NEW MEXICO. The city owes both its existence and its name to the Atchison, Topeka & Santa Fe Railroad. In 1907, when the Santa Fe built a siding at the site for switching freight cars, the first residents were the railroad hands who operated and maintained the siding. Naming the place was a simple matter for the crew: to keep their foreman in good humor they dubbed it Riley's Switch in his honor. A few years later Riley's Switch achieved importance when the Santa Fe built repair shops there and established it as a major shipping point for ranchers and farmers in the region. With its new importance, Riley's Switch came to the attention of many people who previously had not known the place existed, among them the daughter of a Santa Fe executive. Snobbishly, she turned her nose up in disdain at a place-name that honored a foreman when there were so many more distinguished figures to memorialize. Culling her list of candidates, she selected Clovis, a king of ancient France, and her indulgent father ordered the change made.

DISPUTANTA, VIRGINIA. With the arrival of the 1850s came a realization among citizens of the community that they ought to adopt a place-name for the first time. Everybody had his own idea of what the village should be called, and no two ideas were the same. The dispute over a suitable name dragged on for weeks with no end in sight. Finally, since the only point of complete agreement was that their name was in dispute, the residents concluded that the only possible solution was to call the place Disputanta.

DODGINGTOWN, CONNECTICUT. Although it is quiet and sedate today, behind its peaceful exterior lies a stormy past. In pre-Revolutionary days the town was notorious for its roughnecks and scalawags, and constables discreetly gave it a wide berth. Consisting mostly of taverns and crude inns, the place was an ideal hideaway for conmen and rogues who were on the dodge from the authorities, and they flocked to it like homing pigeons whenever the police were after them. However, nothing lasts forever. In time the inns became empty, the taverns dried up, and law and order came to town. But the legends if its "dodging town" past remained alive and were perpetuated in its name.

DUBLIN, TEXAS. In the fascinating world of place-names, things are often not at all what they seem to be—there is nothing Irish about this Dublin. The first permanent settlers were so consistently harassed by hostile Indians that they build a large, double-walled, log enclosure in which to gather for their mutual protection whenever the Indians were on the warpath. When they took refuge in their double-walled enclosure they said they were "doublin' in" for safety. So frequently were they "doublin' in" that the settlement came to be known widely as Doublin. When a town council was eventually formed it found itself confronted with a place-name that was less desirable than it wished but was too well entrenched to discard easily, so the council masked its humble origin by eliminating the *o* from its spelling.

EARTH, TEXAS. It was an act of nature that gave this hamlet its name. At the very moment that the villagers had gathered together to try to determine what to call their community, a violent sandstorm sprang up. Contemplating the thick cloud of wind-borne soil swirling around them, they found the inspiration for their name.

EMBARRASS, MINNESOTA. Two centuries ago French fur traders industriously plied the nearby river in their continual search for beaver pelts. Negotiating the river at that point always presented hazards to the traders because the watercourse cork-screwed in a series of bends that trapped floating driftwood. More than one trader lost his furs when his canoe was holed by a driftwood obstruction. Because of the ever-present driftwood, the French named the site Embarrass, "obstruction." The town that developed at the site assumed the place-name that the French had coined, and ever since then travelers have been puzzled by it.

ERIE, PENNSYLVANIA. The U.S. Army officers who laid out the city in 1795 had both a sense of justice and a flair for history. Their sense of justice led them to select an Indian place-name for the city because the area had long been populated by Indians. Their flare for history directed them to the one name that was peculiarly appropriate for the site—Erie, for the Eriez tribe. The Eriez had been the original inhabitants of the area, but 150 years earlier the entire tribe had been massacred by the Seneca. So it was white men who resurrected the Eriez from the dead, at least in name, after they had been wiped out by fellow Indians.

FITZGERALD, GEORGIA. It usually comes as a surprise to discover that only thirty years after the Civil War—when the wounds of that bitter tragedy were still raw—a Northerner founded this Southern city in an unusual effort to heal those wounds. It all started with a serious drought that struck the Midwest in 1894. Despite the fact that his own state still suffered from the devastation it had sustained during the war, the governor of Georgia dispatched a trainload of relief supplies to help ease the crisis his former enemies faced. Impressed by this act of generosity, P. H. Fitzgerald—an Indiana lawyer and newspaper publisher—conceived a plan to bring Northerners and Southerners together. He bought 50,000 acres of Georgia land to create a city especially to attract veterans of the Union Army as well as native Georgians, believing that former enemies living and working side by side would lose their animosity and distrust as they learned to regard each other as neighbors and friends. Laying out the city on a grid pattern, he named the streets on the east side for Union generals and those on the west for Confederate generals. The four streets bordering the central square he named for naval vessels, two of them Confederate and the other two Union. The residents themselves named their Northern-Southern city for Fitzgerald.

FLAGSTAFF, ARIZONA. Because the site had abundant firewood and a constantly flowing spring, it became popular in the mid-1800s as a camping ground for trappers and for pioneers heading farther west. On July 4, 1876—the nation's one hundredth birthday—a group of Army scouts who were camped at the spot decided that because this Independence Day was so special it called for a special kind of observance. Selecting a tall pine tree that grew apart from the others on the highest point in the vicinity, they shinnied to its crown, lopping off all the branches as they climbed. Then the scouts lashed an American flag to the top of the tree. Travelers became accustomed to using the homemade, prominent flagstaff as a landmark, and when a permanent settlement developed there a few years later it adopted its best-known feature for its name.

FORTY FORT, PENNSYLVANIA. Nearly 200 years ago a detachment of soldiers was assigned to establish a fortified strong-point for the protection of settlers scattered through the broad valley. To make certain that he overlooked nobody, the detachment commander took a census among the settlers he was charged with protecting and found that they numbered exactly forty families, whereupon he named his strong-point Forty Fort. The town that grew up around the fort retained its name.

FRONT ROYAL, VIRGINIA. Before the Revolution the town was a popular way station for frontiersmen heading into the wilderness to the west. Intent on having one last fling before plunging into the forest, the frontiersmen raised so much drunken mischief that the settlement was known as Hell Town. Life in Hell Town became more disciplined during the Revolution when English troops marched in and occupied it. To keep his soldiers from becoming soft and sloppy during their uneventful occupation, the commanding officer drilled them daily in a clearing dominated by a giant oak tree that had been dubbed the Royal Oak. To line his men up for their daily drill, the commander called out, "Front the Royal Oak!" Military commands have a way of becoming pared down to their essentials, and eventually he abbreviated his order to "Front Royal!" When the war had ended and the town was being chartered in 1788, its citizens had no wish to revert to the Hell Town it had been, so they agreed to stay with the words they had heard daily for so long: Front Royal.

GARRYOWEN, MONTANA. The name recalls a sad moment in American history. Situated near the point where the Big Horn and Little Horn Rivers join, the town overlooks the spot where Lieutenant Colonel George A. Custer and 211 of his troopers of the 7th Cavalry Regiment were surrounded and wiped out by a combined force of Sioux and Cheyenne on June 25, 1876. The town that developed near the scene of the tragedy commemorated that mournful event by christening itself Garryowen for the ancient Irish tune that was the regimental song of the 7th Cavalry.

GNADENHUTTEN, OHIO. The Mohicans who founded this town in 1772 were a new kind of Indian. They had been converted to Christianity by German missionaries, embracing their new faith with enthusiasm and sincerity. In choosing a name for their town they sought something that would accomplish two objectives: express their affection for the German missionaries, and reflect the fact that they had become Christian Indians. With a superb sense of the precisely appropriate, they selected Gnadenhutten because it is a German word and because it means "tents of grace" and thus creates an atmosphere of religious belief while at the same time it suggests Indian tepees.

HAVRE DE GRACE, MARYLAND. The town's three-hundred-year history commenced when it began life as simply a rest stop for stagecoaches plying the post road between Baltimore and Philadelphia, and was called Susquehanna Lower Ferry for the nearby ferry spanning the Susquehanna River. A small community slowly grew up around the rest stop. In 1785 Lafayette, who had passed through Susquehanna Lower Ferry several times during the Revolution, described the place in a letter to a friend as a *havre de grâce*—a "haven of charm." The residents learned of Lafayette's description of their community. They were so flattered and pleased by it that they at once renamed themselves Havre de Grace.

HELENA, MONTANA. In 1864 four prospectors who had been searching fruitlessly for gold returned to a gulch they had previously prospected to take one last chance at hitting pay dirt there. This time luck was with them and they struck it rich. A crude, lusty town sprang up quickly and—not unexpectedly—dubbed itself Last Chance. During the months that followed a number of more polished families arrived to take up residence in the rapidly growing town. The newcomers considered Last Chance a crude, jarring name, and they called a town meeting to select a more fitting substitute. One of the newcomers proposed to the audience that they style the community after his hometown of Helena, Minnesota. The rough-and-tumble miners were willing enough to go along with the choice but they refused to accept the Minnesota pronunciation of He-LEE-na. They insisted that the pronunciation in Montana had to be HELL-ena. So the town got a more genteel name but with a less genteel sound and each side came away feeling victorious.

HOP BOTTOM, PENNSYLVANIA. The name seldom fails to amuse and puzzle tourists. But the settlers who chose it for their community nearly two centuries ago were seeking neither to amuse nor to mystify. All they were doing was acknowledging the most prominent physical characteristic of the site—the masses of wild hops growing in the bottomland along a nearby creek.

HORSEHEADS, NEW YORK. A weary, hungry detachment of

troops under General Sullivan encamped here for a time during the Revolution. The quartermaster rations on which they depended failed to reach them and the grim prospect of slow starvation became a very real threat for the men and their horses. Finally, because they could see no other way out of their predicament, the soldiers butchered and ate their horses, leaving the heads in a field where they were picked clean by buzzards. The field with its mournful crop of horseheads became firmly fixed in local legend and was later given permanence when it was commemorated in the name of the town established near the site.

HUBBARDSTON, MASSACHUSETTS. Back in the mid-1700s when the residents were debating the question of what to call their town, one made a proposition to the others. "Name it after me," he said, "and I'll provide a set of windows for the town hall at my own expense." Glass at that time being both costly and scarce, his thrifty neighbors closed the deal with him. The town was christened Hubbardston and Thomas Hubbard, keeping his end of the bargain, wrote off to Boston for a set of glazed windows to be charged to his account.

INK, ARKANSAS. The score of families who lived in a hamlet in a bend of Arkansas' Quachita River were annoyed by the tiresome trek they had to make each day to pick up their mail from the nearest postal drop-off point. They believed they had as much right as anyone else to enjoy mail deliveries, and so they petitioned the authorities in Washington to establish a local post office for them. The federal officials were agreeable to the request but they were stymied when they tried to decide what to call the post office because the village had never got around to choosing a name for itself. To decide the matter in democratic fashion, the Post Office Department sent each family a questionnaire on which to indicate its choice for a place-name. Heading the form was the admonition: PLEASE WRITE IN INK. Heeding the words more literally than Washington had intended, a majority wrote "Ink" and the hamlet had its name. By a curiously appropriate accident of geography, Ink is located only a dozen miles from Pencil Bluff, Arkansas.

JACKSON, NEW HAMPSHIRE. There is nothing especially surprising about an American town that was named for a President, for scores of them exist. But Jackson is different from all the others. Unlike the rest, it was named for two Presidents. In 1800 when it was established, the founders christened it Adams in honor of the second President, John Adams. Events progressed routinely in Adams until July 4, 1829, when the town staged a rousing Independence Day celebration. Stirred by the patriotic speeches, the free-flowing rum punches, and the crackling fireworks, the municipal fathers decided that they ought to cap the excitement of the day with something that would have lasting impact. Giving free rein to their imaginations and rum cups, they conceived the idea of renaming themselves from Adams to Jackson for the man then occupying the White House, Andrew Jackson.

JELLICO, TENNESSEE. Most of those who first settled the site were related to one another and the hamlet was known informally as Smithburg for their family name, Smith. But after the village had grown large enough to apply for official incorporation the residents decided they needed a designation with more formality and significance than Smithburg. They considered the matter and agreed that the Biblical Jericho would suit their purposes very nicely. However, in making out the actual charter of incorporation a clerk who was both a poor speller and a poor student of the Bible misspelled Jericho as Jellico.

JIGGS, NEVADA. When the community was established in the mid-1800s none of the founders could think of a place-name that suited everybody. A name would be adopted, disagreement over it would persist, and soon it would be dropped and another substituted in its place. But nothing put an end to the disagreement. The town embraced and then discarded a series of titles—among them Mound Valley, Hilton and Shelton—without finding the means of shutting off the long-running argument. The continuing discord was upsetting to the postal authorities in Washington because they were in the process of opening a local post office. But every time they thought they had its name nailed down the townspeople had a change of heart and switched to something else. One of the postal officials, convinced that the residents would never come to a lasting agreement among themselves, decided to take matters into his own hands. A man with a sense of humor and a fondness for the comics, he arbitrarily named the town Jiggs because Maggie and Jiggs in that popular comic strip—like the residents of the town—were forever arguing with one another.

KING OF PRUSSIA, PENNSYLVANIA. The initial settler was a German immigrant who opened a tavern and hostel to cater to the needs of travelers. As a mark of his regard for the ruler of his native land, he named his tavern The King of Prussia. The name later expanded to also designate the community that eventually grew up around the tavern. (Many another American town has similarly assumed its name from a tavern that had been the seed of its growth—including, in Pennsylvania itself, the towns of Bird in Hand, Red Lion, and Blue Ball, and in next-door Maryland another Blue Ball and a Rising Sun.)

KOSCIUSKO, MISSISSIPPI. Traders from the hill country of Kentucky had long floated down the Mississippi in flatboats carrying their goods to merchants in Natchez, Mississippi, far to the south. On the return to Kentucky they were forced to go overland because the current of the river was too powerful for them to row against on an upstream course. Their route back to Kentucky led them over the Natchez Trace, a trail hacked out through a damp, swampy, heavily forested area paralleling the river. In 1806, President Thomas Jefferson ordered that the Trace be widened and improved to provide for military usage and to serve as a mail route. A mail station called Red Bud Springs was established along the widened Trace. Gradually the station became a town whose residents were not quite satisfied with their place-name—what they really wanted was something with more bite to it, something of more significance that people would note and remember. They decided in 1836, when they were in the process of incorporating the town, to rename it for a Revolutionary War hero. The difficulty was that a great many places had already beaten them to the punch—all of the notable figures of the Revolution had already been claimed, many of them several times over. Then one resident thought of Tadeusz Kosciuszko under whom his father had once served. The rest of the town gulped collectively—not because Kosciuszko's Revolutionary War contributions were not meritorious but because his Polish name was an uncomfortable mouthful for them to pronounce and an awkward handful for them to write. But there was no denying that no other town had yet claimed him and that he was a genuine hero. Facing up manfully to the challenge, Red Bud Springs switched to the Polish name, making only one change by dropping the z from Kosciuszko.

LANCASTER, MASSACHUSETTS. The farming community there petitioned the Massachusetts General Court in 1653 for incorporation as Prescott. The court angrily rejected the petition as an affront to all Massachusetts. What stirred the magistrates to anger was not that the farmers wished to become incorporated as a municipality, but that they wished to honor their local blacksmith by naming the town after him. The magistrates delivered a haughty rebuke that it was "unseemly that a blacksmith be honored ahead of his betters," pointing out that no town in the colony had yet been named for a governor. The farmers had no alternative but to discard their wish to honor the popular blacksmith. On the other hand, they were determined to ignore the very clear hint that they style themselves after a governor. Instead, they cannily chose for themselves the name of Lancaster, England, figuring that the magistrates could not very well reject the name of a city in the mother country. It turned out that they were right.

LA CRESCENT, MINNESOTA. The town was built on the Minnesota side of the Mississippi opposite the Wisconsin city of La Crosse, and from the very beginning there was friction between the two. Those on the Minnesota side of the river were convinced that the Wisconsinites opposite in La Crosse looked down their noses at them as Johnny-come-latelies. To show their defiance of La Crosse, the Minnesotans adopted the place-name of La Crescent because during the Crusades the Crusader banners borne by the Christians were marked with a cross while the banners of the Moslems who resisted them were marked with a crescent. It was some years later that the Minnesotans learned that the Crosse in La Crosse was in reality the name of one of its founders, rather than—as they had supposed—an indication of the Christian symbol.

LANGTRY, TEXAS. The crossroads hamlet's most famous citizen was a love-sick saloonkeeper who was also a part-time judge. Judge Roy Bean, who was widely known as "the only law west of Pecos," operated his court in his barroom with a six-shooter in one hand and his only lawbook in the other. In actual fact Bean was merely a justice of the peace, but he was the only representative of the law in a rough-and-tumble area, and he took his responsibilities seriously, dispensing an off-the-cuff brand of justice that made the punishment fit the crime. Bean was also very serious about one other thing—the great passion he felt for Lillie Langtry, an international stage star of the period. The deeply smitten saloonkeeper-judge sent her countless love letters, none of which she answered. Even though he was a spurned lover,

Bean could not put the actress out of his mind. He called his saloon "The Jersey Lilly" for the popular nickname of the object of his affections (misspelling Lily by giving it an extra "l"), and the town itself he christened Langtry for her actual name. And, of course, he continued to write love letters that went unanswered. Intrigued by the man who had worshiped her from afar for so long and who had named both his town and his saloon for her, the actress became curious to see what her faithful admirer looked like. Between stage engagements in the United States in 1904 she decided to pay a surprise visit to him. Unknown to her, Judge Roy Bean had died just a short time before her special train arrived in Langtry.

MALAD CITY, IDAHO. French trappers ranging through the region in their persistent search for valuable pelts made camp at the site and became painfully sick after drinking from the river that flows past it. Carefully marking the river on their maps, they named it Malade Rivière—"sick river"—as a warning to others to beware of the water. Settlers arriving from the East years later established a town on the riverbank. Unaware of the meaning of the waterway's name—which by now had become a fixture— they derived their municipal title from it, thus putting "sick city" on the American map.

MARVIN, SOUTH DAKOTA. Initially this was simply an equipment siding on a railroad grade, and the rail hands who were its only permanent residents christened it Grade Siding. But in time other people and other businesses came to Grade Siding and it began to achieve a certain measure of local importance. By 1882 the town had grown sufficiently to rate a post office of its own, but the federal authorities, finding Grade Siding too crude a name to suit them, ruled that the office would not be opened until the residents adopted a satisfactory substitute. So the citizens gathered at the rail depot to try to devise a new municipal title that would suit Washington. It was heavy going until one of them, with a flash of good-humored inspiration, called out, "There's a safe name if ever there was one," as he pointed to the manufacturer's nameplate on the depot safe. Grade Siding borrowed its new name from the Marvin Safe Company and got its post office.

MERINO, COLORADO. When permanent settlement commenced there over a century ago the buffalo were everywhere one looked and in recognition of the great herds the community called itself Buffalo. Then, in the 1870s, the professional hunter began to pay increasing attention to the beasts so thick in places that it was said—in exaggeration that did not do too much violence to truth —that you could walk until your feet gave out without once touching ground simply by stepping from the back of one animal to the back of the next. Coldly efficient hunting machines, the buffalomen decimated the herds in their greed for hides for sleigh robes for the giant market back East. In only a few years the herds had become dramatically—and sadly—thinned out. Now a newly imported animal began to be seen where once the buffalo had stood shoulder to shoulder. Sheep. As rapidly as the buffalo had diminished, so rapidly did the sheep increase in numbers and in economic importance. So, in 1881, the people of Buffalo abandoned the fading beast they had named themselves for and became Merino for the variety of sheep being raised all around them.

MUSCLE SHOALS, ALABAMA. There is a fifty percent chance that Muscle Shoals is the wrong name for the town and for the Tennessee River rapids from which it derives its municipal title. The name goes back two centuries to the time rivermen began using that term when they spoke of the rapids. It was never clear whether the rivermen coined the term because it required strong muscles to paddle through the powerful rapids or because mussels were found in abundance along the riverbed. When the name began to appear in written form the writers spelled it as either

Mussel Shoals or as Muscle Shoals, depending upon which account of its origin they believed. In 1892 the U.S. Board on Geographic Names settled the matter—although, perhaps, not accurately—by arbitrarily ruling that "Muscle" was the official version.

NEW BRAUNFELS, TEXAS. Prince Karl zu Solms-Braunfels had much in common with the fictional Don Quixote who tilted at windmills. The German Prince Karl, like the Spanish Don Quixote, was an impractical daydreamer whose visions of accomplishing great deeds were out of touch with reality. In 1845 Prince Karl obtained a leave of absence from his post as an officer in the Austrian Imperial Army, gathered together two hundred Germans, and led them to America to create a new city in the New World. The place Prince Karl chose for his mighty endeavor was a site in south-central Texas. His first act after arrival was to erect a fortresslike log headquarters on a hilltop with a commanding view over the countryside. Then he raised the Austrian flag over his headquarters and staffed his command post with velvet-clad aides. He himself usually wore his splendid, gilt-decorated, Austrian Imperial full-dress uniform, especially when there were Indians in the vicinity. The glittering splendor of his uniform impressed the Indians but did not deter them from harassing the settlers. Prince Karl's grand project bogged down. Disillusioned and unable to adjust to the harshness of frontier life, he gave up and returned home after one year of reverses and frustration. But most of his German followers remained, endured the privations and perils, and triumphed over them to create a flourishing city that Prince Karl zu Solms-Braunfels had been able only to dream of. Having made a reality of the dream, they erected a place-name monument to the dreamer by styling themselves New Braunfels.

NOME, ALASKA. Although the English never attempted to establish a colony in Alaska, the region for a long time held a great fascination for them and attracted scores of Englishmen to explore its mysterious, frozen vastness. In the late 1700s a survey party aboard the English vessel *Herald* was industriously engaged in charting a long sweep of previously unexplored Alaskan coastline. The survey teams worked ashore each day, returning to the *Herald* in the late afternoon to turn over their day's accumulation of notes and sketches to the draftsmen to transcribe onto master charts. One afternoon one of the surveyors turned in his work, an exploration of a coastal cape, and to remind the draftsmen that the cape had not yet been named he penciled "Name" on his sketch. This particular surveyor was scrupulously precise in his sketching but sloppy in his handwriting. The draftsman cannot be blamed for reading "Name" as "Nome" and for carefully lettering his misread word onto the master chart as the designation for the cape. Maps that were later printed from the chart made the mistake permanent. In 1899 when gold miners built a city on the cape they adopted for it the name that had been created unwittingly by a surveyor who wrote in a scrawl.

OIL TROUGH, ARKANSAS. One of the reasons settlers were attracted to the site was the presence of numerous bears and the realization that bears could be a lucrative cash "crop." They hunted the bears in the surrounding woods, hauling in the carcasses to be butchered and boiled down to render out their thick larding of oils and grease. Then they felled trees and hollowed out the trunks to form troughs they filled with the rendered oils. After they had filled enough of the wooden troughs to make it worth their while, they lashed them together to form a raft which they floated downriver to New Orleans where they sold the contents for cooking and industrial use and for hair "stick-em." When it came time to choose a name for the settlement they figured it was no more than simple justice to memorialize their thriving business by calling the place Oil Trough.

OLD HICKORY, TENNESSEE. For over a century the city was named Jacksonville for Andrew Jackson who had lived nearby. And in all that time the residents had fumed with annoyance because the mail intended for them was constantly being delivered in error to other Jacksonvilles scattered across the country. They knew that they could put an end to their frustrating situation by abandoning their place-name, but they cherished Andy Jackson and they would not give him up to cities that they felt had less of a claim to him. Finally, in 1923, they conceived a shrewd way to rid themselves of their problem without relinquishing their hero to others. They voted to rename themselves Old Hickory, for Andrew Jackson's nickname, secure in the knowledge that there was not another city anywhere styling itself in that way.

OLD TRAP, NORTH CAROLINA. A lusty, hard-drinking waterfront settlement, this was also a marketing center for farmers of the surrounding countryside. The rough gaiety of the taverns after the loneliness of their farms and the barkeep's liquids were irresistible magnets for the farmers. Invariably, after disposing of their crops, they made the rounds of the taverns. Eventually, nursing a hangover and whatever remained from the sale of their harvest, they found their way back to their farms. Their wives angrily dubbed the settlement The Trap. The name took hold and in time became modified to Old Trap.

PARIS, KENTUCKY. Grateful for the aid France had rendered to the United States during the Revolution, those who founded the town soon after the war named it for the French capital. Then, thinking the gesture perhaps not sufficient to indicate the depth of their gratitude, they named their county Bourbon for the Bourbon kings who sat on the throne of France. With that out of the way, they devoted their time and talents to practicing a skill at which they were masterful: making corn whiskey. The fame of their Kentucky corn whiskey began to spread far and to gain converts. Soon, to make sure that they were getting the genuine article, people began calling for it as "bourbon" after the county in which the Paris whiskey-makers produced it.

PAROLE, MARYLAND. During the Civil War many draftees in the Union Army who had no stomach for fighting intentionally maneuvered themselves into positions where they were easily captured by the Confederates. They had a purpose in doing this. They knew that by pledging their "parole" to the Confederates— their promise never again to take up arms against the Confederacy—they would be freed by their captors to make their way back to their homes as best they could. The Union Army, well aware of this trickery being practiced by some of their men, picked up those suspected of the deception when they reentered the North and shipped them to a prison camp in Maryland. The prison was called Camp Parole—for its "parole" prisoners—and after the war the town that developed there retained the place-name.

PAWHUSKA, OKLAHOMA. During a skirmish between an Army detachment and a band of Osage, the detachment commander sustained a relatively minor wound that momentarily stunned him and caused him to topple from his bucking horse. A young brave, glimpsing the officer's long, remarkably white hair, galloped up intent on obtaining the prize with his scalping knife. The brave grasped the hair but before he could swing his knife the officer dashed away and leaped on a riderless horse, leaving the astonished brave gaping at the hair in his hand. Never having seen a wig before, he was convinced it possessed a secret power enabling it to come away in his hand so magically. The splendid wig became his most cherished possession, and from that day on he wore it constantly, earning him the name of Paw-Hu-Scah, "white hair." Paw-Hu-Scah eventually became a prominent Osage chief, and when this was established as a tribal town it was named for the chief with the long white hair.

PENN YAN, NEW YORK. Two separate groups migrated to this point in the Finger lakes region of upper New York in the late 1700s. Each group, while not precisely distrustful of the other, was nevertheless on the alert to see that the other did not gain any undue advantage. This continual jockeying for position was usually kept under control but threatened to get out of hand when it came to deciding what to name their community. One group—New Englanders proud of their heritage—insisted that the only fit name for the settlement was Yankee. The second group, migrants from Pennsylvania who were no less proud of their own heritage, insisted the name of the new settlement had to be Pennsylvania. There was a deadlock until someone conceived a compromise that was acceptable to each side. The first syllable of each proposed name was used to form Penn Yan.

PIE TOWN, NEW MEXICO. The tiny hamlet was born nearly fifty years ago when a prospector settled at the site to work a small mining claim. The claim failed to pan out and the prospector concluded that the smartest thing he could do was to lay aside his pick and shovel and find a better way of making a living for himself. Attracted to the automobiles that were commencing to take to the roads in appreciable numbers, he decided to open a garage to serve motorists passing by on U.S. 60. In between customers there were long periods of idleness; to fill his idle hours, the prospector-turned-garage-owner began to practice a skill he had acquired earlier: baking pies. To supplement income from the garage, he hawked his pies to the drivers who stopped at his gas pumps. The pies were so flavorsome that it was not very long before they, rather than his garage, were the lure that attracted drivers to his door. It was inevitable that the community's sole claim to fame would create its place-name.

PLANT CITY, FLORIDA. In deference to the tobacco they grew locally, the Indians who were the original inhabitants called the site Ichepucksassa, "place of tobacco blossoms." The whites who later came along found that the name was a bit more than they could handle and began to look for a substitute. The community's first postmaster, an Irishman, saw his opportunity; he arbitrarily named the town Cork after his birthplace in the Old Sod. It remained Cork until the South Florida Railroad laid its tracks to town in 1884. Then, grateful for their new rail connection, the residents voted to change to Plant City in honor of Henry B. Plant, president of the railroad. It turned out that the name was unusually suitable because the town developed into an impor. 'nt agricultural center.

POCATELLO, IDAHO. Just over a century ago a section of Idaho tribal land evoked envy among the directors of a railroad. Not unduly greedy, all the directors wanted was permission to run their tracks through the land and to establish a railyard along the way. Pocatello, a member of the tribe, offered his services to the company—for a price—in influencing his fellow Indians to decide in favor of the company. The offer was speedily accepted. Pocatello knew how to present his case in the best possible light and he was successful in securing the tribe's permission. Overjoyed by the success of their go-between, the directors named the railyard after him. The railyard grew into a town and eventually it dawned on the residents that they were saddled with a somewhat unsavory place-name; the dawning came with the discovery that Pocatello means "not to follow the path" and that the tribe had bestowed it on the man for whom the town was named because he seldom went straight.

PUNXSUTAWNEY, PENNSYLVANIA. Indians knew this site well, but they wisely gave it a wide berth in summertime. Their caution stemmed from the fact that each summer the site swarmed with vicious little gnats called "ponkies"—ashes—by the Indians because their bites stung like the burn of hot ashes. The place itself the Indians called Ponki's Utenink, "place of the ponkies." But if the place had its summertime ponkies, it also had a thick stand of timber and rich coal deposits. Attracted by those valuable resources, whites had tried for years to settle at the site but always, when summertime rolled around and the gnats swarmed, they were forced to retire in defeat. However, in the early 1800s a determined group of settlers moved in and waged all-out war against the ponkies. The route to victory was painful for the settlers, but ultimately they eliminated the pesky gnats and were able to get their lumbering and mining operations under way. In tribute to the opponent who had held them at bay for so long, they retained the Indian place-name, modifying it from Ponki's Utenink to Punxsutawney.

REFORM, ALABAMA. Established as a farming community in 1817 by newcomers from South Carolina, for the first few years it got along without a name. The farmers worked hard, and when their chores were light they played hard, and between the two they had given little thought to a place-name. Then, just when they were beginning to give the matter serious consideration, a fiery, circuit-riding preacher came to the settlement to conduct a series of revival meetings. The preacher delivered his sermons passionately, pleading fervently with his congregation to confess their sins and mend their ways or burn in the eternal fires of damnation. His final sermon was especially passionate, and it moved many in the audience to rise to their feet and publicly confess their sins. Before he left town the preacher was asked for his advice in naming the community. Pointing out the number of residents who had admitted sinning, the preacher said only one name was suitable—Reform. His advice was heeded.

SACRED HEART, MINNESOTA. The first permanent resident came on the scene almost 200 years ago to establish a trading post for Indian furs. The most noticeable thing about the trader who ran the post was the great bearskin hat he wore summer and winter, indoors and out. Among the Indians the bear was considered to be a sacred animal; they referred to the trader's headgear as "the sacred hat" and to the post as "the place of the sacred hat." In time a hamlet developed around the trading post, and it too came to be known by the Indians' designation for the post. Sacred Hat. But uninitiated travelers invariably assumed the name was actually Sacred Heart and persisted in speaking of the place in that way. The persistence of the travelers won out over the patience of the residents and in the end they changed the hat to a heart.

SALEM, MASSACHUSETTS. Almost from the arrival of its first families in 1626 the town was split by discord and dissension. In the beginning it took the form of bickering about land boundaries. Then it broadened to include disputes over the way the local authorities were administering the town's affairs. After a half-century of this kind of turmoil, the situation took a more ominous, brutal turn when a wave of religious fanaticism washed over the community as neighbor accused neighbor of practicing witchcraft. For a dozen years the town was gripped by this madness that culminated in the infamous Salem witch trails. In those trials more than twenty persons charged with witchcraft were either hanged or died in jail. Then the fanaticism petered out and sanity and tranquillity came to Salem. The irony is that the the residents had named their community Salem from the Hebrew word "shalom," meaning "peace."

SHOW LOW, ARIZONA. The two original settlers were C. E. Cooley and Marion Clark who, after seeing each other day after day with nobody else to break the monotony, began to get on one another's nerves. Mere annoyance with each other deteriorated into outright hostility. Realizing that the breach between them could not be healed, the two former friends agreed to play a game of Seven-Up, the loser to pack up and move on. After a few hands, Cooley needed only one more point to win. Clark drew his cards and ran over. Tossing his hand down in disgust, Clark said, "Show low and you win." Cooley triumphantly turned up his hand, saying, "Show low it is." Clark moved on and Show Low it remained for the community that in time emerged there.

SISTERSVILLE, WEST VIRGINIA. Charles Wells arrived with his bride in 1802 to homestead there. The ground was fertile and Wells worked hard to make the most of it. His successful farm attracted others, and soon a lively agricultural settlement had grown up around the Wells homestead. In the meantime, Mrs. Wells was proving to be as fertile as the land. Each year, regularly as clockwork, she bore another child and each time it was a girl. When the twentieth girl was born the Wellses marked the occasion by christening her Twenty; in all they had twenty-two daughters. In 1839, when the village had become large enough to create a local government, it did not take the villagers long to choose their municipal title. Nothing would be more apt, they agreed, than to dub themselves Sistersville in recognition of their most notable local crop—the Wells sisters.

SWANSEA, SOUTH CAROLINA. Although its name gives no hint of it, the town was established by German immigrants. Practical people, they called their community Zwanzig—"twenty"—for the quite logical reason that it was exactly twenty miles distant from the state capital, Columbia. There was trouble with the name from the very beginning. English-speaking South Carolinians could appreciate its practicality but they were hard-pressed with the challenge of pronouncing and spelling it in the proper German manner. So, in a spirit of friendly accommodation, the founders of Zwanzig made things easier for their neighbors by modifying their name to the more manageable Swansea.

TAOS, NEW MEXICO. For almost a century this city has been known by a name to which it is not legally entitled. Its actual, proper title is Fernando de Taos, conceived to honor both Don Fernando de Chaves, an influential Spaniard who was one of its early residents, and the Taos Indians who were the original in- habitants. But in the 1880s the local postmaster—who fancied himself an efficiency expert—reasoned that his work would be simplified if everything were dropped from the post office name except Taos. He notified his superiors in Washington of his brain- storm and they approvingly and arbitrarily redesignated the post office as simply Taos. The abbreviated name came into general use although no official body has ever initiated the necessary procedures to rename the city legally. (If Taos has been sailing under false colors for nearly a century, Hackensack, New Jersey, persisted in a similar voyage for two and a half centuries. It was not until 1921 that the city of Hackensack gained the legal right to the name it had been using since 1664. In all that time the city's actual, official name—which it never used—was New Bar- bados, bestowed on it in 1647 by the Dutch traders who had come up from the Caribbean island of Barbados to found the town as a mercantile base at a site the Indians had called Hack- ensack.)

T.B., Maryland. For brevity and oddness, few American place-names are in quite the same league as this one. When strangers pass through town they usually expect to glimpse at least one sanitarium somewhere along the route, but this T.B. was not inspired by tuberculosis. It came into being because the town was laid out on land that had previously belonged to Thomas Brooke. A cautious man who did not believe in leaving things to chance, Brooke posted boundary markers at closely spaced intervals all around his land to ward off trespassers. Each of the scores of markers carried his initials imprinted on it in large letters to make sure that nobody missed the point. The founders of the town, so accustomed to seeing the T.B. initials all about them, preserved the familiar marking as their municipal name.

Temple, Pennsylvania. The residents found themselves confronted by a problem when they considered what to call their community. For a long time the most popular place in the little town had been the King Solomon Tavern. Because they regarded the tavern so fondly they were in agreement that it should be memorialized in the town name. On the other hand, they realized that civic dignity required a choice that suggested something more lofty than a tavern. So the problem was one of deciding between what they wanted to do and what they felt they ought to do. After mulling the dilemma for a while, they arrived at an ingenious way to memorialize the King Solomon without suffering any loss of civic dignity. They simply adopted the eminently respectable name of Temple because it was King Solomon who had built the Great Temple in the tenth century B.C.

TEN SLEEP, WYOMING. The Indians had devised a graphic way of describing long distances—less precise perhaps than the white man's miles but it got the point across. They reckoned distances in terms of the amount of ground a horseman riding at a steady canter could cover in one full day of riding—in other words, the ground he could ride between sleeps. Because it required ten days of riding to reach Fort Laramie from there, the founders of the settlement called it Ten Sleep.

TOMBSTONE, ARIZONA. When Ed Schieffelin made up his mind to prospect for silver in this area in 1877 he was either braver or more foolhardy than many another prospector; he was fully aware this was Apache territory and the Apaches meant to keep it so. A friend of his, emphasizing the likelihood that he would be killed by the Apaches if he persisted in his plan, warned Schieffelin that his reckless disregard of the perils facing him would get him a tombstone instead of a silver mine. But Schieffelin was obstinate. He went ahead with his prospecting, managing not only to stay alive but to strike the silver he was seeking. When he registered the claim, he dubbed it Tombstone in good-natured heckling of his cautious friend.

TROY, NEW YORK. The Indians who planted corn here long before the arrival of the first white settlers called it Pa-an-pa-ack, "field of standing corn." There was some talk among the settlers of perhaps modifying and retaining the original Indian place-name for the community they were creating. But one prominent Dutch resident, Jacob Vanderheyden, was dead set against it. He wanted the town named Vanderheyden for himself, and he tried to twist arms to obtain agreement. But most of the people in town were opposed to both the Indian and the Dutch name, considering each to be too unwieldy. Over Vanderhyden's outraged objections, they adopted the short, crisp Troy for the ancient city in Asia Minor. During the War of 1812, the Army's rations were poor and—even worse—their distribution was haphazard so that soldiers were usually ill-fed or unfed. However, in the Troy area things were different. Soldiers stationed in the vicinity were regularly provided with plenty of fresh meat by Samuel Wilson, a Troy butcher. Tales of Wilson's faithful, generous regard for the soldiers spread throughout the Army and soldiers everywhere praised the butcher whom they affectionately dubbed "Uncle Sam." Long after both the meat and the war were forgotten, Uncle Sam had become firmly established around the world as an American national symbol.

TWO DOT, MONTANA. In the cattle country of the West and Southwest a rancher's branding iron was almost as important and as well known as his name. Consequently, a number of communities drew the inspiration for their place-names from their most prominent, local brand mark. This accounts for Two Dot's name as well as for the names of places like Kaycee and Jay Em, both in Wyoming.

VIRGINIA CITY, MONTANA. The discovery of gold here during the Civil War caused a sudden influx of miners bent on making their fortune. Like so many other Americans of the period, their wartime loyalties were divided, some sympathetic to the Confederate cause and some dedicated to preservation of the Union. A group of the Southern sympathizers gave tangible evidence of their loyalties by naming the hastily built town Varina for Varina Davis, wife of the president of the Confederacy. However, they had reckoned without the man who had been appointed judge of the local court, which put him in a position of considerable power. A Northerner, the judge considered Varina to be an affront to everything he believed in. Adamantly ignoring Varina, he began heading all of his official documents "Virginia City," ruling that by his decision that had become the official name of the city. Although the Southerners were annoyed to have the judge discard their choice, they could hardly object to his substitution since Virginia was a leading Confederate state, and so they accepted it. What the Southerners did not know was that the Virginia for whom the judge had named the city was not the state; the Virginia memorialized by the judge was an old sweetheart of his.

WAUSA, NEBRASKA. The Swedes who founded the town had immigrated to America only a short time earlier. Nevertheless, they had already discovered that Americans mispronounced foreign words. They agreed they would name their town for King Vasa of Sweden, but they also agreed that no American would give Vasa its proper Swedish pronunciation. Having great affection for the place of their birth, they were determined not to cause King Vasa to become Americanized out of shape. To prevent that from happening, the town's founders craftily adopted the subterfuge of deliberately misspelling Vasa as Wausa. The result is that when native-born Americans pronounce Wausa in their normal fashion they are actually giving King Vasa's name its authentically Swedish sound.

WHY NOT, NORTH CAROLINA. When the time arrived to select a name for the community the residents gathered in their local general store to consider the matter. Each time a place-name suggestion was offered someone else would counter-propose "Why not name it so-and-so?" The hour grew late and still each suggestion was greeted by a fresh "Why not name it this-or-that?" Finally, nettled by the indecision and anxious to go to supper, one man called out, "Why not just name the durned place 'Why Not' and be done with it?" The rough-hewn logic appealed to the audience, and the suggestion was adopted.

WILMINGTON, DELAWARE. Thomas Willing was a man who wanted to become wealthy and it seemed very likely that he would achieve his goal because he had a knack of responding when opportunity knocked. In the early 1730s he formed a syndicate to lay out and develop a city on a parcel of land that was available in Delaware. Since he was the dynamo making the wheels turn, the city was named Willington in his behalf. The project went well from the start, rapidly gaining residents and businesses. In 1736 Willing was immersed in plans for the construction of a farmer's market in the heart of town, but another enterprising citizen of the community, William Shipley, recognizing its potential for profit, stole a march on Willing by quickly building the market himself. Willing was furious. Sputtering with rage, he went ahead with his plans anyway, building his market only two blocks away from Shipley's. The rivalry between the two market-owners was intense and it affected the rest of the town, dividing it into pro-Willing and pro-Shipley factions. Hitting on a scheme to strike a blow against the Willing camp, Shipley and his supporters began to agitate to eliminate Willington as the town name. Naturally, the Willing camp fought the move. The situation was brought to the attention of William Penn, proprietor of Pennsylvania, whose jurisdiction at that time also extended to what is now Delaware. Penn astutely devised a solution that enabled him to kill three birds with a single stone. He issued the city a charter in the name of Wilmington. This honored his old friend, the Earl of Wilmington, Bird Number One. The Shipley forces had been clamoring for a change and they got one, so that constituted Bird Number Two. But Wilmington was so nearly identical to Willington that the Willing supporters were able to maintain that no change at all had been made. Bird Number Three.

WINONA, MINNESOTA. This was never intended to be a city. It started out as Captain Orren Smith's private woodyard. Smith, captain of a paddlewheeler plying the upper Mississippi, was disturbed because so much of his valuable cargo space had to be used to carry wood to fuel his vessel's boilers. It dawned on him that if he had a refueling point ashore at a midway point he could take half of his on-board wood storage space and devote it to revenue-producing cargo. So in 1851 Smith put some crewmen ashore at a densely forested site to fell trees and establish a woodyard for the vessel. His action opened the eyes of others to the potential of the heavily wooded spot. Several families settled around the woodyard to begin lumbering and sawmilling operations. The community prospered and the residents decided to formalize their existence by selecting an official place-name. The name they chose was Montezuma—for the Aztec emperor—but almost at once they felt uncomfortable with it, finding it a bit too elegant for a lumberjack's down-to-earth taste. So they selected Wenona—the name Sioux families traditionally gave to their firstborn daughter—but they altered the spelling to Winona to give it a touch of individuality.

YONKERS, NEW YORK. The city started out as a farm settlement on a grant of land held by Adrien Van der Donck, the first lawyer to hang out his shingle in the Dutch colony of New Netherlands. Because Van der Donck was a member of the Dutch upper class, he was customarily referred to as "jonker"—your lordship. The community of which he was the ranking resident came to be called The Jonker's Town. After New Netherlands passed to English control and was redesignated New York, the English energetically substituted their own place-names for

Dutch ones but found that The Jonker's Town had become too firmly entrenched for them to end its use without a great deal of effort. So the English contented themselves with merely shortening it and Anglicizing the spelling to Yonkers.

YOUNG AMERICA, INDIANA. In the 1850s when the town was established, much of the nation was caught up in an aggressively patriotic movement that visualized the United States as playing a leading political and economic role on the world stage. The movement—called "Young America" and supported especially by Democrats—pushed for expansion of the nation, gave encouragement to European revolutionaries seeking to overthrow their home governments and replace them with a republican structure, and urged the lifting of all barriers to free international trade. The town's founders, enthusiastic about the Young America movement, thought they could do a whole lot worse than to name their community for it.

Index of Place-Names

The Author

Vernon Pizer is a free-lance writer, based in Washington, D.C., who has published five books and more than 300 articles in major publications in this country and abroad. Mr. Pizer entered the Army in World War I, serving in North Africa and Europe, and retired from military service as a lieutenant colonel in 1963. He has traveled extensively, and his one objection to writing is that it takes time from his favorite pastime of fishing.